THE YEAR I ATE MY YARD

THE YEAR I ATE MY YARD

ESSAYS FOR THE VEGETABLE GARDENER

With a Foreword by Emily Green

MASTER VEGETABLARIAN

www.Vegetare.com

P.O. BOX 91002
PASADENA, CA 91002-1002

Although the author and publisher have made every effort to ensure the accuracy and completeness of information contained in this book, we assume no responsibility for errors, inaccuracies, omissions, or any inconsistency herein. Any slights of people, places, or organizations are unintentional.

First Edition 2005

Edited by Pamela Staley Herr
Foreword by Emily Green
Designed by Susan Panetta
Cover art and all photography by Tanna Herr

ISBN 0-9752869-0-0

Library of Congress Control Number: 2004110307

TO TANNA
As the strawberry loves the sun and showers

and

TO PAM
As the strawberry needs the sun and showers

With loving memories of
Sally Ann

and the Grampas
Ed, Jim, Gene and Bob

CONTENTS

ACKNOWLEDGMENTS

House on fire! You finish a book and then you sit back with a steaming cup of burned-bean water and you can't help but be knocked flat by the myriad of people who have helped in one fashion or another with your manuscript's production. So buckle up, I'm going to thank a boatload of extraordinary people here.

Tanna, thank you for every day past, present and future. To Pam, my editor, cheerleader and personal de Medici— immeasurable, profound thanks. Susan Panetta, my word, what can I say but thank you so very, very much. A whopping gracias grande to my ever-clever blood-sister and the most delightful garden guru that I know of, Emily Green. To Steve Martin, Marilyn Diamond and Sharon Gilmore-Reilly thank you again for your kind words and friendship.

A googolplex of merci beaucoups to family and friends, colleagues and associates who've allowed me to bounce all sorts of wackiness off of them and have given their precious time, their invaluable knowledge and their stories to this project. Love and thanks to Cara and Jackson, Allen and Marge Kienitz, Bart Bernstein, Don, Julie and Rachel Herr, Carey (AKA Eddie Peenie), Steff, Mike, Jake and Ben Ells, Robin, Nancy MacDonald, Tom, Paul, Keliy, and Emily Staley, Patsy and Denny Meudt, Stephen and Terri, Suzanne and Ed, Dave, Elaine, Steve and Tracy Kienitz, Linda, Dick and the Jensen clan, Jim and Jean MacDonald, Marty and Mary and their brood, Nettie, Janet and Jared, Marjorie and Alexandre. And of course, Zuzu and Tahoe.

Big, big thanks to Catherine Downes, Gary Jones, David Diaz, Scott Daigre, Steve Gerischer, Jennifer and Appie Vanderfluit, Mark Bartos, Barbara Hogan, David Gregoire, Matt Dell, Mark Hansen, Andy Olson, Ilene Waterstone, Jim Walker, Bryant Arnett, Eric Hi3ll (the three is silent), Frank Burkard, Vince Razo, Linda Persson and Gary Butters, Sean Hawkins, Kim Gosney, Celia Bonaduce,

Descanso Gardens, the Huntington Gardens, the L.A. Botanical Gardens, the Learning Castle, Pie Town Productions, Screen Door Productions, the Pasadena Showcase House of Design, Don Schlossman, Cindy Davidson, Karen Castle, Adamo Schell, Hunt and Betsy Burdick, Jan Smithen, Mike and Bob Hipolito, John Schulian, Erin and Matt King, Kathy Siegel, Gary and Joanne Hunt, Susan Kranwinkle, George and Marilyn Brumder, Emily Young, Hector and Cindy Aristobal, Kenneth and Kathleen Daffner, Sally Faulkner, Marcia Rorty-Greenfield and Stephen Greenfield, Timmy, Billy and Annie Carruthers, Regina Stewart, Billy Hart, Kerin and Jen Lifland, Bonnie Saland, Raffi Alexander, Brenda Rees and Jim Hughes, Malcolm, Andrea, Darla and Chris MacDonald, Tom and Maureen Reed, Palma and John Vincente, Diane Curran, Susan, Jane and Bob Wachsler, Michael and Melanie Yonks, Zsa Zsa Gabor, Jack LaLanne, Ren Hanami, Mr. Nick Tan—thank you all. Lastly, enormously and always, thank you Tracy and Time Winters.

FOREWORD

I love Tony Kienitz's gardens, but I only sort of understand Tony Kienitz himself. Insofar as I do, it was an accidental epiphany. His family was over for a dinner party and his son, Jackson, met up with the daughter of a neighbor, another three-year-old, Lydia. While the adults chitchatted amiably enough, Jackson and Lydia were soon inseparable, running this way, running that, Jackson leading, Lydia following, a trail of chatter hanging in their wake.

It sounded like babble. However, during one of the duo's streaks through the kitchen, past the sleeping dog, into the garden, I noticed Jackson, then Lydia, stop to pet my dog. Until she linked up with Jackson, Lydia had been so afraid of dogs, she had to be carried around them, even my docile Labrador. Jackson had taught her how to approach the retriever, show her hand, read its reaction, pat it. Jackson, I realized, was like Tony – a born teacher.

So if you read this book, prepare to be grabbed by the hand, and brace for the chatter. Tony doesn't so much organize his thoughts about gardening as riff on them. It's tempting to blame the sun. Few other Southern California gardeners are so proud of where they come from, so aware of how localized good garden writing must be, or more thrilled by it. "Brandywines struggle in Chatsworth," he writes. "Beans love Riverside. Peppers love Culver City. Cukes like Compton. Lettuce likes Laguna. You get the picture."

Well, you might not right away, but all will become clear. In that instance, he's discussing microclimates, but in a tumble of words, not zone numbers. He's a popularizer whose ideas just keep bubbling up. Here's how you construct a garden bed . . . don't recycle your newspaper, use it as mulch . . . here's how you make a rebar tomato cage . . . if you must kill bugs, kill them by hand . . . pet your plants.

I don't agree with all of his advice (I like Algerian ivy – so do lizards). I admire pigeons (he hates them). I pull the weedy volunteers that sprout every year after the city street palms go to seed (Tony eats them).

However, when he's right, I feel those rare surges of envy that only well up for those we profoundly admire. My favorite part is when, enjoining us to garden, he says, give it twenty minutes a day. Only twenty minutes, and then he evokes the paradise those twenty minutes will create. Other gardeners recommend planting thyme. Tony knows better. He tells us to tuck it in everywhere.

His ideas are part horticulture, part art, and part world-according-to-Tony. Some are borderline kooky, some are sound, but they are all born in the garden. The garden, above all, is Tony's kingdom. Anyone who has seen his gardens couldn't fail to be moved by them. I am still looking for a spot to create a swirling stone and gravel path, interspersed with California poppies like the one Tony did one year for the Pasadena Showcase House of Design.

Tony isn't typical and this isn't a typical garden book. It races along in language of a man almost talking to himself, which gardeners will recognize as an afternoon's deep thoughts rolling around beneath a broad-brimmed sun hat. At the same time it's full of great advice. Half way through, he submits to an organized impulse, and pelts an alphabet of interesting information, starting with tidbits about artichokes and concluding with zucchini, Zulus and Zsa Zsa Gabor. At some point, he remembers, "Paper coffee cup sleeves, the kind you'll find at just about every coffee shop, are perfect for protecting new transplants from cutworms, snails, slugs and other crawlers."

My advice: buy this book, take it to a coffee shop, and remember the Godard quip about one of his new wave movies. "It has a beginning, middle and end, but not necessarily in that order." Read the parts that interest you, skip the parts that don't, and then, before leaving, steal a stack of those coffee cup sleeves. You'll be needing them.

~ Emily Green, Los Angeles, July 2004

"The real cathedrals are the
cathedrals of nature."

Dr. Helen Caldicott

THE YEAR I DIDN'T EAT MY YARD

I began eating my yard several years ago. Initially, I thought, I'd grow enough food to equal 75 percent of what I ate daily and then dutifully document the process. I felt, and I think rightly so, that if anyone could live in an urban setting and pull off the challenge of raising enough fruits and vegetables to survive on, it would be me.

In the beginning, I attacked the project with an imperialistic passion. I grew twenty kinds of tomatoes, all the lettuces one could want, five bean varieties, okra, sesame, radishes (black, red and white), carrots, beets, chard, sorrel, peas, amaranth, eggplant, onions, garlic, shallots, leeks, potatoes, brussel sprouts, broccoli, broccoli raab, sunflowers, Malabar spinach, black Italian cabbage, red cabbage, emerald cross cabbage, loufa, parsnips, peanuts, mallows, red shiso, burdock, black-eyed peas, marijuana (not really, just seeing if you're still reading this list), collards, artichokes, chervil, oregano, rosemary, thyme, parsley, grapes, loquats, apples, oranges, lemons, cantaloupe, pumpkins, raspberries, sage, blueberries and more. I did not plant hundreds upon hundreds of the same kind of anything — rather, just a few of everything, which, to my way of thinking would provide me with a plateful of something different every day of the year. Y'see, I live in Pasadena, CA, and my growing season never ends. There are only brief intervals when plants struggle to survive — January and the thirty days between August 15 and September 15. Plants don't die then; they just shuffle along like ancient widowers with swollen ankles, sore hips, deep coughs and no-good lottery tickets. My plants don't grow many leaves during these periods, but they do continue to produce edible offspring. We often pick tomatoes on New Year's Day. Steinbeck maintained that California is the land of milk and honey, but I gotta say it sure seems more like the land of fruits and vegetables to me.

If anyone could raise enough in his own back yard to live on, it should've been me.

I mowed into the project with tremendous energy, but within a month I was floundering. I wasn't accustomed to writing it all out. When I did sit down to write, my entries did not teem with excitement and intelligence, no, rather, they just, in a word, sucked. "Boy-ar-dee! I've been eating my own micro-greens and I've lost four pounds!!" "Oops, I slipped up and let the bindweed grow up the sunflowers." "Today it was, like, really hot." Not electrifying material, to be sure. Yes, I was looking at a stack of writing that validated book burnings.

I was also surprised to discover that while it was simple to produce all of this bounty; it was a royal pain in the arse to drag myself out to the garden to harvest it. And then, my word, how exhausting, I had to wash it and chop it and spice it and cook it before eating it. How primitive! How annoying! Within a month I'd returned to the stupidity and convenience of frozen pizzas.

I needed to change my habits, my perspectives and my expectations if I were ever to succeed at growing my own. Consequently, I would begin "The Year I Ate My Yard" three times. The resolve and purpose I'd adopt at the outset would slowly erode, and again, I'd be back at the starting block. Each renewed attempt did bring a different Tony to the task, however. Slowly, I began to get with the program. I didn't know where I was going but going I was.

And then a moment came on one hazy summer afternoon, the sky bleached and the dirt hot to the touch, when the garden gave me something I hadn't asked for. Something more than sustenance. Something deeper. I have read many accounts of spiritual awakenings in my time, experiences that alter the way one perceives life. Dan Millman wrote of a mind-bending experience in a eucalyptus grove next to Stanford University. Antoine de Saint-Exupéry met with truth in a fighter plane above Arras. Others have fasted for a glimpse of understanding, have momentarily died and seen the light at the end of the tunnel, or have folded their legs lotuslike and sat for years beneath a bodhi tree. My moment came while weeding.

Prepare yourself now, because this is <u>not</u> the most momentous insight you're ever going to read. In fact, it's not an original insight at all—many have perceived this before me. But it was <u>how</u> it came to me that gave it special meaning to me. I was weeding yellow dock and cheeseweed in one moment and in the next found myself seeing every object as glowing, shining, slick with light. It didn't happen instantly. No one had hit me with a flat-blade shovel (as far as I know). Honestly, I can't remember it beginning, but as I knelt in the dirt, I found the weeds in my gloves, the soil, the air, my eyelashes, and my skin, everything to be glistening. So I stood slowly, tried to shake the cobwebs out, walked over and sat in the shade of a pecan tree and wondered if I were coming down with something. I was slightly alarmed by what I was experiencing but, oddly enough, I also found myself laughing. For a good half an hour everything shimmered like dawn on a wild lake. And then a thought came into my head, but it wasn't my voice, wasn't my inner voice, it wasn't any kind of sound I'd heard before, it was formless, without words yet quite clear, "It's all God."

And that was it. That was my moment and I was high all day. The next morning I was back to normal, but that day, wow. It was all God. God as Creator. God in the Christian sense, the Buddhist sense, the horse's sense. God is the word that my mind chose as a way of describing everything, but it just as easily could have been "Brad" that came to my mind and the truth would have had no less impact upon me. If I'd heard, "It's all Brad," I believe I still would have understood.

I have found that when I can hold onto the concept that all is God, my experience perfects itself. When I allow myself to feel every particle of every thing as being created, then I am filled with an immeasurable quiet and a playful, chuckling happiness. I walk through the garden smiling, realizing that there is not, cannot be, any separation between what is. Everything that is, is created. Even nothingness, a vacuum, a void, is created. It's all God. Every piece of you and me is God, and there's nothing we can do to change that. The Source creates from itself and cannot take itself out of what has been created without eradicating itself and that it cannot do. It's all God, and it's all in God's image. It could not, to my mind, be any other way. And as scientists seek to find the beginning of the universe they choose to ignore that the universe could never really begin because it can never truly end. Reduce the universe to a speck of dust, and it is still an entire universe within a speck of dust. Reduce it further, infinitely, finally to nothing, and still there is something, for nothing is still something. God simply is and is simply everything. And that, to me, makes everything sacred. Too easy? For some, yes. Perfect nonetheless? For me, thankfully, that would be affirmative.

After my "moment in the weeds" I had a place to launch a project from. I began to view the garden and my relationship to it differently. I began, in a connected way, to see that our societal habits were soiling our soil, fouling our seas and gassing our skies and that something had to be done to stop it. I began to see that when I began to repair my partnership with the other living things in my yard then the world began to heal a tiny bit, too.

What you'll be reading here is not the end-all how-to vegetable book. Rather, I hope to share with you why we need to grow.

"I'm not a vegetarian because
I love animals; I'm a vegetarian
because I hate plants."

A. Whitney Brown

MASTER OF MY OWN DOMAIN

Our house is plagued by pigeons, which, I suppose, is proof we live in a city. Scores of potential squab call our eaves their roost, and they leave their graffiti everywhere. Pigeons are the living scourge of my days. My appreciation of nature is vast and I strive not to separate myself from nature at all but these DAMN BIRDS!! To make matters worse, an old woman down the block, a woman who'll never understand the ritual horror she inflicts, scatters seeds for the pigeons every sucking morning. They don't roost and poop on her house, no, they just act pretty over at that address.

So, I throw rocks at them. Gravel. Tennis balls. I even bought a wrist rocket slingshot ($8.32) and have pelted a few slumbering rascals with that but, ultimately, nothing works. They just fly over to my neighbor's roof and strut about like pot-bellied Euro-dads in black Speedo swimwear. The damn beasts mock me. They wait for me to go back inside. They don't stress. They have all the time in the world. A sexagenarian feeds them. Why should they worry? They can loiter all they want. Friggin' birds.

Where I've wired over the eaves (a rather comely look for any home I might add), the pigeons just cling to the galvanized mesh screen for hours at a time, leaving poop streaks in new and even more exotic locations daily. They'd rather be slightly uncomfortable than go looking for new digs. They can't be bothered.

Overall, not in any way to sugarcoat my feelings . . . I despise pigeons.

Okay, now the other day, as I was cleaning up the back forty, I gazed up at the cursed bird remnants painting the house like so many Picassos, and there I saw, settled onto one of the beams, the beginnings of a nest. Quickly, angrily, smoke curling out of my ears, I grabbed a ladder. I was not about to have another generation of these creatures homing back here, no ma'am, I was going to destroy that nest. I climbed the ladder, reached up, and grabbed the nest. Poop and dust came splashing down so I shut my eyes, held my breath, and scuttled back down the ladder. When I opened my eyes I found a pink and blue featherless chick in the nest, one unblinking black eye staring back at me passively, almost zen-like, as if saying, "I am in the Now, how 'bout you brother?" A single unhatched egg lay beside the chick. "Oh, great." I thought about it awhile. "Well, I'll just kill it." But how? Drown it? Snap it? Put it in a plastic bag and let it suffocate? Bury it? I had to do something with it because it wasn't going back up into the eaves. No way, no how. Not a chance in Hell. But, but, y'see, I couldn't kill it. The more I thought about how I might kill it, the more difficult the idea of doing it became. And all the while I mulled, the fragile life I held within my hands peacefully awaited my decision.

I was reminded of my friend James, who was a member of the Special Services. While in training, he and others, as an exercise, parachuted into a remote desert with some water, a knife and a rabbit. They were required to find their way to a designated area fifty miles away within three days. It was recommended that they kill the rabbit immediately after hitting the sand because if they didn't, and the rabbit was allowed to become a pet, well then, they'd barely be alive by day three. James inadvertently killed his rabbit when his chute opened up, but many of the other trainees couldn't kill their rabbit. Many failed the mission because of it. My mission was to rid our house of pigeons, and I was about to fail.

I ended up by doing possibly the cruelest thing of all, merely because I couldn't stomach doing anything else. I placed the nest in the tall foxtails on our parkway in hopes that one of the 'hood cats would take care of business for me. I walked away from the nest knowing that it would haunt me the rest of the day. And so it did.

But the lesson was and is about connectedness. As a society and culture that adores eating meat, we most always forget that the flesh we eat was once alive. I used to say and think that it was okay for me to eat meat because I could kill and slaughter the animal. Now I don't think I could, and now I don't eat meat. The way the world works today, I don't honestly think many of us could kill and slaughter a pig—or a cow—or a chicken. I think the number of people who could and would kill is enormously smaller than the number of people who think they could. We are so removed from nature that we can, in our lifetimes, individually, consume hundreds of animals and never once really know that we took a life. We can eat without thinking. We can eat without respect. We can take a mother's child, eat it, and never, not once, honor the animal that gave its life to sustain us.

I wonder if it would be appropriate for all sixth or seventh graders in the U.S. to engage in the slaughtering and dressing of a chicken as part of their curriculum? I mean, shouldn't they experience the truth in some way? We slaughter millions of chickens each day—it could easily be arranged to let junior high kids in on the party, wouldn't you think? It's not like there are not enough chickens to go around. I think it would be educational for the kids and illuminating. But I also accept, of course, that it will never happen. If a soldier can't kill a rabbit, our kids wouldn't be able to kill chickens. It would be inhumane to require them to do so. No, better to close our eyes and, much like me with the baby pigeon, just hope that someone else will do the dirty work for us.

A follow-up note on the pigeon chick—I found it dead the next day, shriveled like a peat bog corpse in the ragtag nest, one bony wing draped protectively, or so it seemed, over the unhatched egg lying intact in the nest. There was a poetic beauty to the brave little chick's final act. It made my heart squeeze in on itself. Days later I found the same egg in my backyard, drained and hollow, carried there, I'm certain, by the immense raccoons that roam our neighborhood, emerging nightly from the storm drains and striding down the streets as tough and ominous as any gangbanger. In the end, this is what I get for my inability to kill the baby pigeon, or for not leaving the nest undisturbed. Instead I've got raccoons big enough to kill my dogs—dogs goofy enough to run out and challenge a bandito raccoon to a lethal game of tag if I'm not ever watchful.

During the Middle Ages the people of Europe executed countless cats. They believed, as taught by their church, that cats were servants of Satan. The brethren killed Muffy and Socks and their ilk in such an efficient manner that cats nearly disappeared from the European continent. Consequently a gargantuan explosion in the rat population beset Europe. It was the rat equivalent to the Baby Boom. The Rodent Rumble. Along with the rats came the Black Plague, and we all know about that little bit of history. No cats, lots of rats, and dat's dat.

In nature everything is interconnected, one thing always leads to another in a perfectly elegant manner, but unfortunately it doesn't always play out in a way one can predict. I live in a city, a city of over one hundred twenty-five thousand citizens, in a metropolis of over three million, in a county of nearly ten million, in a region of the world populated by thirty-four million. Even here, amidst all of these people, nature can still make me humbly aware of how omnipotently present it truly is.

Each and every action I take in my garden has consequence. I think, "what will happen to the lady bugs if I spray the aphids with a paraffin oil?" "Does the chlorine in my water kill the good bacteria in my soil?" "Is this fish emulsion a by-product of an industry gone mad. If so, should I be using it?" "Where did this bone meal come from and what practices am I supporting by buying it?" I try always to respect the bigger natural picture for fear that if I don't some new dilemma is going to come swinging in on me from the other direction and I'll be in a tighter pickle than ever before. Staying attentive to the warp and woof of life helps me avoid learning lessons the hard way.

Palma's Grandma's
Old Country Recipe

Cut leaves away from some chard and chop
the stems into bite-sized pieces.
Parboil the chard. While you're boiling you
can mix together a batter of:

> *One or two eggs*
> *Garlic (lots)*
> *Grated Parmesan*
> *Olive oil*
> *Salt*

Stir the chard into the batter and let it sit while
you sip wine or pick the kids up from Greco-Roman
wrestling practice. Later, put your battered chard
into a skillet with some olive oil and cook it up.
Serve it hot.
Eat.

THE ONLY REAL RULE

Credit this to Flip Wilson . . .

There's this city guy, right? And this particular guy goes out and buys a brand new Maseratti. Red. Shiny. Fast. Man, that car could FLY! Fly like the wind. But, but, but this city guy, he's got nowhere to drive it, see. Nowhere to kick it into gear, let it loose, let it FLY! So, he's a smart fella, thinks to himself, "I'm gonna drive it out to the country. Open her up on a country road. Wide open spaces. Yessir, that's exactly what I'm gonna do." And so, don't you know, that's just what he does.

And now he's in the countryside and he's FLYING! One twenty, twenty-five, ONE HUNDRED THIRTY miles per hour. He's a red blur. He's driving so fast that his lips are pulling back on his face in a crazed monkey grin. Fast, man, fast. The boy is FLYING!

And then . . . Kachunk! Kupper, kupper. "What's that?! Oh hell, what's that?" Kachunk, pittuh, pittuh, pittuh, ssssplahhhh. The car dies. Dead. Just gives it up. The guy can do nothing but coast to a stop. Stops on this country road, middle of nowhere, not another soul in sight. Guy gets out, cussing and crying, lifts the hood. His beautiful red Maseratti is D.O.A. dead.

Now, this particular guy knows a thing or two about a thing or two but he doesn't know the first thing about cars, see. He could stare at that engine for the rest of his days and never figure out the least of it. But, still, 'cause he's a guy, he's gotta lift the hood. He knows that much.

So, he's staring at the engine, cussing to himself, crying, frettin', and suddenly he hears this voice,

"It's the alternator."

The guy jumps back from the car, scared outta his wits, looks around, sees no one, quickly spins around the other way, no one. He rubs his head, pinches the bridge of his nose. When he turns back to the car,

"I'm tellin' you, it's the alternator."

Now, NOW the guy is spooked. Thinks maybe he shouldn't have had that piña colada with lunch, or maybe he should've had more piña coladas. Doesn't know what to think. Slowly he peers around the hood of the car and what does he see but an old grey horse standing on the other side of the barbed wire fence calmly staring back at him. And the horse smiles cordially and says,

"No doubt 'bout it, it's the alternator."

Well, the guy takes off. He DASHES outta there. I mean, DASH. Like he was faster than that new car of his. DASHES over the hill, around the bend, three miles in three minutes. The guy just runs like the bejesus. Until, up ahead, he sees a farm. And there's this old farmer taking his mail out of the box and the city guy, with this rooster tail of dust following him down the road, he runs right up to the old coot in a panic,

"Mister, mister, my car . . . my car . . ."

"Now hold on there feller. Catch your breath 'fore you go on hollerin' in my ear."

"My car . . . broke down. Along the road . . . there . . . and . . ."

"You need a ride into town? Guess my daughter could give you a ride. I can't drive no more on account of my thrombosis."

"No, no. There was this . . . horse. He . . . he talked to me. I'm dead serious. He said, 'It's the alternator.' I am not making this up."

"Horse, huh? Grey horse, with a swoop back?"

"Yeah, yeah. That's him!"

"This horse got a white circle round one eye?"

"Yeah, yeah. That's him. Mister, I swear he said, 'It's the alternator.'"

"Horse sorta look like he just woke up?"

"Yeah, yeah, that's him."

"I knows that horse son and, well, son, that horse, you don't want to be listening to him. He don't know nothing about cars."

If I told you that the <u>only</u> thing you need to do to grow superb vegetables is to build up superb soil you probably would run away spooked outta your gourd or you'd choose to totally ignore me based on the advice of some old farmer.

People write long books devoted to the proper care and feeding of vegetables, each type of crop given its own chapter, each plant its own list of rules. But hey, we arrogant writers needn't really go to all that trouble and you honest gardeners really don't need to read every word.

Tend the soil. Add composted matter until you have deep rich loam. You can turn it thoroughly, double-dig it (as John Jeavons recommends) or, if you're not in a hurry, you can just pile stuff on top—eventually the soil will improve. If you can create a closed-system microenvironment, your battle will have been won. Truly, the better the soil, the better your success in the garden will be. The highest quality soil will always produce the highest quality plants. Admittedly, once you've built great soil, there are other tricks of the trade to optimize your rewards, but if you're looking for simplicity, then the level truth is prep your soil, plant your seeds, water if you don't get rain. That's all, folks. You can stop reading now if you'd like.

"Results! Why, man, I have
gotten a lot of results.
I know several thousand things
that won't work."

Thomas Edison

THE THOUSANDTH LIGHT BULB

It took me years before I realized that Jimmy never accepted dinner invitations. He would not eat at someone else's house for the life of him. I finally had to ask why, and this is what he told me . . .

When Jimmy was in his teens and the lead singer of our high school's most popular garage band, he, as required by his position in life, wore his hair long and longer. His hair curled down over his shoulder blades, he could sing, play a lick or two, and had an earring made from a fishing lure (a pink rubber squid) gracing his lobe. Jimmy rocked.

One day Jimmy was invited to have dinner at Bryant's house. Bryant's family came from the Midwest (or simply, the Mid, as I like to say) and although at first blush you might assume them to be squares, you'd be woefully wrong, because they were distinctly rhomboid, perhaps even a touch cubic. Nevertheless, Jimmy felt he had to be on his very, very, very best, *Leave It to Beaver* behavior for the meal. Jimmy dressed smartly, washed twice, said please and thanks, never spoke with his mouth full, didn't burp or pick his arse. To his great relief, Jimmy made it through a superb dinner without committing the slightest faux pas.

At the end of the meal, as family members leaned back, pushed their plates away, crumpled up their napkins, Jimmy stood and began collecting the dishes. Bryant's mother told Jimmy he needn't do it, he was their guest, she would get them. Jimmy insisted. And as Jimmy bent over to pick up the gravy boat his rockin' long hair swung forward directly into the candles and instantly went aflame like the Olympic Torch at opening ceremonies. Jimmy hopped about screaming, "Tito, Tito!" while Bryant's entire family jumped him and applied various fire-fighting techniques and strangleholds.

Dazed, embarrassed and slightly aroused by Bryant's mother's mouth-to-mouth resuscitation, Jimmy vowed never to eat at another family's home again. And for years he ardently kept that pledge.

And then along came Linda.

Linda was Jimmy's first great love. They went together, by teenage standards, for a long time. When Linda begged Jimmy to join her family for Thanksgiving at Gramma's, Jimmy found it impossible to turn her down. So he went. Dreading it. Obsessively battling his dinner demons. He fretted and paced and stewed about the event for weeks. And then the day arrived. And the men footballed. And the women stuffed. And the men drank. And the women snuck cookies and pie.

Midway through the feast all seemed good for Jimmy. Nothing imaginably disastrous loomed on the horizon, and it appeared he was going to make it through without mishap. He relaxed a little, wondered, "What'n the hell was I so worried about?" He smiled, nodded at a joke, took a bite of salad and a lettuce leaf got caught in his throat. It didn't just get caught, it plastered itself much like a bumper sticker to that part of his tongue right below the epiglottis, right at the spot where every nerve in your body barks out the command to gag! He began to convulse and rasp uncontrollably. Several goblets of water would not wash down the leaf – it only clung to his tongue more tightly. No amount of throat clearing helped – coughing, fingers down the throat, nothing. Jimmy staggered about emitting every freaky sound a human can make and some that we can't. Witnesses were heard to describe the sounds as similar to "a bull moose passing a kidney stone." Fortunately for Jimmy, just as Linda's Uncle Stu was readying his steak knife and ballpoint pen for an impromptu tracheotomy the lettuce leaf dislodged and fled the scene of the crime.

Watery-eyed, red-faced and woozy, Jimmy left the table never to return to another—at least, not for another long time.

What does this story have to do with vegetable gardening? Let's see, hmmm, there was the antagonistic role of the lettuce, but that has nothing to do with nothing. Indeed, this story's moral is simple . . .

You get what you expect. What you think about will appear.

Please stop living in dread of what might negatively beset your garden. If bugs come, so be it. Deal with it then. Learn from it. But, for goodness sakes, relax. Enjoy. Practice seeing more good than bad. Count your blessings. The more fretting about failure you allow yourself, the more likely failure will visit you. And when you look at it honestly, can you possibly fail? Isn't your vegetable garden a big laboratory to begin with? You can only fail if you adopt an attitude that requires a set outcome. Don't cop a 'tude, Dude. When it is positively impossible for you to know what this next second will bring (WATCH OUT!), how can you pretend to know what will occur many months from now. Besides, in today's big picture, we're not likely to starve if our vegetable gardens don't produce perfectly. There is nothing that can besiege our garden that doesn't make for a terrific story later.

Go. Go have dinner at Linda's grandma's house. Have fun. Make a fool of yourself (as if you weren't a fool already. Right?)

Find a twig

Dissect it. Bark, pith, core.

Imagine all of the little things
inside this twig. Littler still.

Could we have done this?

Imagine what the twig was part of.
Big and bigger still.

Could we have done that?

Impressive, isn't it?

Now, clean your teeth with it.

PRESTIDIGITATION

When I was four years old I lived in a house that no longer exists, on a street that no longer exists. A freeway came through and with a flourish of eminent domain, vanished it all. Thus the powdery bones of my Buick-biting dog, Farner, and the rust of my beloved swing set have now been blown to distant locales by the draft pull of ten million vehicles. Even the land beneath my home, swing, and dog is gone—the excavated roadway running fifty or sixty feet beneath what once was. Sometimes I find it strange to have meaningful memories of a place that no longer physically exists. Otherwise, though, I am grateful to have lost something so precious, so completely, at such a young age. When I was four I learned to love what I couldn't see and to wonder at what was beyond my understanding.

When I was four my best friend in the whole world was Billy Hart. Billy lived up the street a ways. He was a big kid. He was five and a half. He wore a buzz-cut so precisely coifed that people were tempted to conduct land surveys with his head. The kid could wink, snap and whistle. Yeah, Billy Hart was five and a half, he'd been around the block, and he frequently suffered from ennui. He was the king stud of my neighborhood.

Ever so often I was allowed to walk up to Billy's by myself while my mother carefully, so as not to burst my little independent bubble, spied on my progress from behind the juniper shrubs in front of our house. I remember laughing to myself as I trucked along because I could clearly see her cigarette smoke coiling above the bushes. Upon arrival Billy and I would furiously play cowboys and Indians. I was always the Indians (all of them) and Billy was always the lone cowboy fated to a scalping. I spent many a glorious afternoon pouncing out from behind banged-up trash barrels and yanking Billy down into the dust by the short-cropped perfection atop his head. And as if that wasn't enough to keep me in milk-chocolate heaven, sometimes, on the best of days, I was also allowed to have a squaw. Sherry was the little girl who lived in the house next to Billy's. Sherry had ringlets of black hair like the girls in fairy tales and eyelashes longer than a momma cat's whiskers. She was a perfect squaw because she liked to find berries for us to eat. After a long and arduous afternoon of pretending to carve Billy's mane from his skull there was nothing better than sitting down to a Dixie-cup full of purple eugenia berries with Sherry, my devoted squaw. Yes, life was fine. I had a caring mom, a best friend, a squaw and a fictitious mortal enemy. What else could I have wished for? Sherry's grampa had the answer to that one.

One day as Billy rolled in the dirt bemoaning the loss of his forelock while my squaw and I feasted, a rather old man in an oatmeal-colored cardigan approached us from the south. He hobbled towards us shaking things in his pants pockets as only grampas can. Sherry leapt to her feet and ran to him, her buckskin and feathers dancing in the air around her. He picked her up in stride and swung her above his head and over his shoulder and around his back and through his legs and back up to give her a kiss on the forehead. Holy man! Circus tricks?! Billy and I were instantly sprinting up to him and pleading for some of the same. But he begged off by doing an impression of W.C. Fields, "Oh, my suffering sciatica." We continued to plead for a brain-swirling whirl through the stratosphere, but he held up a hand to silence us while his other hand simultaneously withdrew butterscotch candies from his pocket. Before we could snatch them from his clutches he took a single piece wrapped in clear golden plastic, placed it in his mouth, chewed it, swallowed it, digested it slightly and then, and only then, did he reach out and pull the candy out of my ear. He next took another candy, repeated the chewing business and pulled the candy out of Sherry's ear. Then Billy's. Then my other ear. Likewise Sherry's and Billy's. Butterscotch flowed out of our pint-sized noggins, and when I asked him how all of this was possible he answered, gazing fiercely into my eyes, "It's magic, Tony Baloney. Magic is real." He smiled as my tongue chased the hard candy around my baby teeth, as my young mind spun like a dervish, awestruck by the old man's wizardry. It was on that day that I began to believe in magic. Real magic.

Writing about real magic has been difficult to do. Every rough draft of this book has had a chapter on magic, and at every step of the way that particular chapter has always been picked out by my friends and associates as the one piece that could be left out. That chapter has vexed me. When my chum and colleague Nick Tan heard that I might be leaving magic out, he was dismayed. "No way. I've worked with you, what? Almost two years? I'd say magic in the garden is the totality of what you're about. I think you'd be doing yourself a huge disservice if you left it out." He voiced my thoughts exactly. Thanks Nick. I'm going to give it another stab and maybe this time it will stick.

I've realized that the word "magic" has become meaningless in our day-to-day lives. We have magic kingdoms and magic markers and Magic Johnson. I don't know, maybe it's just me, but "getting behind the wheel" of a Mercedes or a BMW has never been particularly magical to me. I've never believed in the magic of floor wax, eyelash thickeners or nonstick muffin pans. In my local yellow pages the word "Magic" precedes many company names. We have a Magic Cleaners, a Magic Fence, Magic Tile, Magic World Daycare, Magic Chef Factory Service, Magic Jump, Magic Nail, Magic Growers, Magic Light Photography, Magic Image and Magic Bevel Leaded Glass. Seven magicians also advertise in our phone book. Sadly, magic has become ubiquitous. Co-opted. Dull.

Writing about magic in the garden is also, let's face it, clichéd. Countless children's stories incorporate the magic of a seed bursting forth, of autumn leaves, of a swallowtail's cocoon. It's no surprise then that adults reading this material were quick to dismiss a meditation on the concept of "magic." I might, too, if I weren't working daily in a fantastical realm—the garden.

Cliché or not, it remains true that the garden is all magic. Here there is illusion, there deception. Kneel motionless for a stretch of time and notice how life re-enters the yard after you've quieted down. Visit a sunflower throughout the day and watch it follow its master like a loyal golden retriever tagging along behind its human—a flower with no musculature, yet twisting and turning, bobbing and weaving. Blur your eyes and see what you were missing— pollen, gnats, sparrows carousing in the bougainvillea—these constant companions are performing outside the scope of our normal focus and they are executing feats of legerdemain essential to future spectacle. Try to smell the heat, the cold, the light. Pick up a stone and notice that nearby there is a pebble that is remarkably similar in shape to the stone—realize that there is likely to be a speck of dust close at hand that also shares contours with the stone and pebble. Gaze at your reflection inside the dewdrop sparkling atop the cabbage. Are those eyes for the cabbages to "see" with? Stand with your feet firmly pressed into the soil and feel the earth's energy streaming through your soles, flowing out through the top of your head and cresting about twelve feet above you. What color is that energy? Violet you say? Hmm, maybe you do believe in magic. Take a leaf from a tree out of the sun and into the shade and gaze at it until you can see its corona. In time the corona will fade, but it is a testament to the life force that it takes so long for the halo to go away. Grab a weed and tell it, with passion, "Thanks weed. You did a good job. Now it's on to compost." Say this first and the weed will pull up quicker than a blouse at Mardi Gras. If there is a breeze, see if you can change its direction for a moment by simply requesting that it do so. Send angry thoughts onto one plant and loving thoughts onto its neighbor—see who's doing better after a week. Politely ask the orange tree which fruit is the sweetest to pick and see if you don't get a great orange every time. Water by hand and visit each plant three separate times. "Thrice watering," as urban survivalists Christopher and Dolores Lynn Nyerges call it, is a mystical practice with a long history. Take a seat in the garden late at night and look for the tiny sparkles dancing in the plants and mulch. A rigorous, scientific mind believes that all I've suggested here are basically just outdoor parlor games or, at best, tricks of the mind. And I say, yup, that's right. Tricks. Illusions. Magic.

Today I stood looking at a spider web and realized that those taut threads anchored from the bay to the macadamia, splitting photons into tiny rainbows as they vibrated to and fro in the breeze were, had to be, making sound. Like a string stretched betwixt empty alphabet soup cans they had to be resonating. I just couldn't hear it. I didn't have the tools, the receptors, the ears to hear. Today there was a storm on the sun and my tomatoes, depressed by it, didn't grow in the least. I didn't feel the sunstorm but the tomatoes did and today my tomatoes were blue. But not my favas. The fava beans that poked through the dusty clay this morning must have, at some fractious moment, exploded into life, creating in their own minute way a spectacular event. Things crashed aside when they sprouted. The event made NOISE! Those favas announced their arrival and told the world to "Watch out! Beans a-coming!" All this in a day. All this magic.

The magic of a garden, and specifically a vegetable garden, is found in daily revelations. There is so much to discover that I can be completely positive that when I am one hundred and thirty I will have barely cracked open the garden's storehouse of secrets. The garden's repertoire is that big. And all of the sleights, the behind the back forces and the twelve-down riffles, the Hindu shuffles and the Mexican turnovers, all happen right before my astonished eyes. The peas bloom, the cherimoya fruits, the world spins, and you and I and the whole lot of us can only throw up our hands and wonder, "How does The Magician do that?"

If I had only experienced broccoli from the market I wouldn't know the baffling truth that broccoli growing beside chamomile tastes better than broccoli living with beets. I wouldn't know that quite magically the blossom end of an orange is sweeter than the stem end, and that fruit from the top branches of the tree are typically better than those from lower branches. Buying lettuce prewashed in "fresh-sealed" bags wouldn't reveal to me that lettuce tastes bitter just as soon as it bolts because the plant, while usually generous with its leaves, can no longer afford to have creatures nibbling upon it. It has to sustain maximum health once it begins to have offspring. Lettuce wants to reproduce itself, acts accordingly, and teaches me to respect it in the process, all without the luxury of language. In order to understand why the lettuce gets bitter I have to communicate with it in a magical way.

Brown onions in a red mesh bag don't explain why they make me cry when I chop them up but those in the garden do. Onions spray out irritants to deter pests, like me, from eating them. The magic of that, to me, is that a simple collection of brainless cells can come up with such an effective and collective defense. The onion fights back when attacked. And that's just the onions. Natural pest deterrents are popping up all over the blooming garden. Scientists are finding that food crops raised <u>without</u> artificial fertilizers and pesticides possess a greater number of antioxidants in their systems (present there to fight off invaders), and if that is true, well then, hooray! my garden is rife with antioxidants. What joy to discover that the less I monkey with the plants the healthier my harvest will be. I can just sit back and watch the show.

There is so much magic going on that it leaves me agog. The garden is the finest illusionist of all, for it allows you to see that it has nothing up its sleeves, isn't using smoke and mirrors or misdirection of any kind, and yet still, out of what appears to be thin, rarified air, it flourishes a bouquet of flowers right before your eyes. Try that David Copperfield.

To watch stage magic is to wonder how a woman can be sectioned into three pieces and still be ticklish. To live with real magic is to wonder where a fava gets its fava from. Living with real magic takes me back to a place that no longer exists in the physical but forever lives in the ethereal. Just yesterday I turned a nine-foot-tall compost pile and while excavating stood inside its 140 degree steam—inside my own dirt sauna. As I toiled there, amazed by the energy of the pile, I had an itch. I set aside my pitchfork, took off my gloves, reached up and pulled a butterscotch candy from my ear. It was delicious.

FAMOUS PEOPLE WHO
ONLY ATE ORGANIC FOOD

Jesus. Buddha. Muhammed. David. Confucius. Sitting Bull. Michelangelo. Cardinal Richelieu. Genghis Khan. King Tut. Louis XIV. Anne Boleyn. Abraham Lincoln. Leonardo da Vinci. Mary Queen of Scots. Cleopatra. Copernicus. Lady Godiva. Aristophanes. Renoir. Rubens. Kubla Khan. Paul Revere. Betsy Ross. Harriet Tubman. Jessie Benton Frémont. Jesse James. Milton. Aristotle. Mary. Joseph. Isaac Newton. Squanto. Ishi. Richard Burton (the original). Nathaniel Hawthorne. Mona Lisa. Caesar Augustus. Thomas Jefferson. Josephine. Victor Hugo. William Shakespeare. Montezuma. Davy Crockett. Molière. Zorro. Christopher Columbus. Eric the Red. Stephen Crane. Martin Luther. Anton Chekhov. Emiliano Zapata. Lord Byron. Mary Shelley. Hippocrates. Pliny. John the Baptist. Chaucer. Wilhem Tell. Grover Cleveland. Billy the Kid. Sam Houston. Sam Adams. John Adams. Toulouse-Lautrec. George Washington. Martin Van Buren. Eli Whitney. Marie Curie. Aesop. Henrik Ibsen. Edgar Alan Poe. Alexander the Great. Charlemagne. Honoré de Balzac. Nero. Lord Nelson. Marie Antoinette. Chopin. Boris Gudonov. The brothers Grimm. Pythagoras. Rembrandt. Yeats. Ramses III. Zoroaster. Rasputin. Christopher Marlowe. James Fenimore Cooper. Fannie Farmer. Anne Hutchison. Fatima. Homer. Franz Kafka. Karl Marx. King Olaf. Shigenobu Okuma. José Rizal. Pope Urban VIII. Tocqueville. Tolstoy. Toledo. George Sand. Otto I. Li Po. Emma Lazarus. Robert E. Lee. Wild Bill Hickok. Annie Oakley. Auguste Escoffier. Francisco Coronado. Francis Child. Cervantes. Amelia Earhart. Pope Innocent III. Harry Houdini. Isabella I. Jean Lafitte. Van Gogh. Josiah Wedgwood. Torquemada. Li Hung-chang. Macbeth. Lao-tse. Mata Hari. Thoreau. Judas. William the Conqueror. Jack the Ripper. Lizzie Borden. Tchaikovsky. Leif Ericson. Lewis and Clark. Euripides. Marcus Aurelius. Archimedes. Charles Dickens. Herman Melville. Salomé. Crazy Horse. Moses. Benjamin Franklin. Goethe. Wordsworth. Emily Dickinson. James Madison. Joan of Ark. Francis of Assisi. Saint Fiacre. Mother Fiacre. Mother Jones. Thomas Paine. Simón Bolívar. Daniel Boone. Adam. Eve. Why not you? Huh? Why not?

LISTENING TO MR. LAMA

A few years ago my wife and I were invited to attend a lecture given by the Dalai Lama. The event was staged at the Los Angeles Sports Arena, and he was reverently introduced to the hushed audience by none other than the Empress of Spiritual Enlightenment herself—Goldie Hawn. Now, I love Goldie Hawn, she was great in Melvin Frank's *The Duchess and the Dirtwater Fox*, but even if she were my closest personal friend I think I'd still find it kind of goofy to have her introduce Mr. Lama. Of course, I couldn't and can't think of anyone better qualified to introduce him. Maybe she was the perfect choice, I don't know. Nonetheless, at the time, I was amused and bemused by Goldie's presence, but that turned out to be only the beginning of the day's wackiness. Folks in our row began to chant and bob and shiver at the mere mention of his, the Dalai Lama's, name. As the Dalai Lama strolled onto the stage a woman wrapped head-to-toe in a single length of purple batik organic cotton fabric, reeking mightily of sandalwood and lotus, stepped into the center aisle and began to writhe and moan unintelligibly. Tears streamed down faces. Hands were pressed to hearts as people tried to catch their breath. All this hullabaloo for a man wearing Buddy Holly glasses and a pumpkin-orange dress.

He quickly put everything into perspective, urging us through his interpreter to remember that he was simply an ordinary man who just happened to be living an extraordinary life. We, too, he reminded us, were living out our own extraordinary stories. He was wonderfully modest, immediately genuine, and had an infectious laugh that rippled through his entire body and sounded entirely school-girlish. You couldn't help liking the dude, that was for sure.

He spoke for nearly thirty minutes about his work and his beliefs before allowing the audience to pose questions of him.

"How do I keep my noisy mind quiet?" asked a teenager with dredlocks.

"Will Tibet ever be free?" queried a middle-aged, balding woman.

"Is it cool hanging out with Richard Gere?" asked Goldie.

"How do I get this monkey off my back? No, really, this monkey isn't mine and it keeps biting my . . . OW! See?!! OW!! Somebody, please help me!!" begged the man with a diapered spider monkey swinging about his neck.

An earnest and clean-cut young man stepped up to the microphone, cleared his throat, and asked, "Your Holiness, what do you suggest we do to save the environment?"

The bespectacled man on stage beamed with joy. Finally, a question he had been hoping for. He rubbed his hands together and giggled. The audience giggled, too. He answered in halting English. He was solemn.

"What I . . . think to do . . . when I go to leave a house . . . and I will tell you this is very good to do . . . when I go to exit . . . perhaps even a room . . . I will make the lights go off. I think, uh-oh, are the light bulbs burning? Then I must make them go off. And I do that for the environment. That is what I do."

"That's it?!" I thought to myself. "That's enlightened?! Geez Louise, how dopey can you get?" His advice was a complete letdown. Talk about anticlimactic. My word.

It took me years to get the Dalai Lama's point. As usual, understanding came to me while in the garden . . .

If I were going to try to save the Pacific Northwest's spotted owl from extinction, I would have the choice of donating money to activist groups who would then try to protect the owls OR I could become an activist myself whose driving purpose was to save the endangered birds and, even more importantly, thwart the nefarious logging company's endeavors by any means possible. Those would be my basic avenues of attack in my quest to save the birds.

The difficulty with getting people to care about anything is that these are typically the only options offered. It's either, "Give us all your money," or "Give us all your finite time." Rarely are we told that by giving a little bit of money and by giving a little bit of our physical being we will be providing enormous benefit to the world at large. So, on a planet where there are too many people, too many causes, too much difficulty in providing simple sustenance or shelter, the response from most of us is inertia. We care, yes. We care about so many things that we can't move, and if we ever do get riled up enough to jump into action we, more often than not, take a slapstick pratfall upon discovering our boots nailed to the floor. The laugh-track roars and we impotently mewl and wail. And once defeated, we begin to make excuses. We tell ourselves that if we only had the money then we could help. If we didn't have two kids then maybe we'd chain ourselves to a giant sequoia in an old growth grove so the timber companies would stop raping and razing the land our kids will someday steward. But those "ifs" are almost never realized. Most of us wish we could. Most of us never do.

But guess what? There is something that you can do. I'm giving you, right now, for a limited time, while supplies last, both option A, money and option B, time. What can you do? Well, to start, you can save a seed.

Think about it. Think a little more, please. If you and a million other folks decide to grow an unusual type of cucumber, that cucumber will be ensured a place in our future. And you don't even have to plant it (but please do). By merely purchasing the seed you are casting your vote for the preservation of that plant. Every time you buy seeds a farmer is sent a message to grow more of those same seeds. Thousands of individuals each buying a unique variety of seed will create the economic impetus to grow a diverse collection of crops and ornamentals.

Turning off the lights is a small step towards saving the environment. Buying a packet of seeds is an equally small step. These small steps must be taken though. To arrive at a healthier future we, each of us, must take care of one little step, every little step, at a time. Turning off lights and buying seeds may be all that we can do to help the bigger reality right now. But we've got to start somewhere. Don't you think?

Andy Olson's Hair

Green, springy and fresh cilantro seeds
Garlic
Olive oil
Half a lemon
Lemon zest
Salt and pepper
Italian parsley
Angel hair pasta

Put on a good bossa nova CD. Cook pasta.
While it's cookin', put chopped garlic, olive oil,
lemon zest and fresh picked cilantro seeds into a
skillet and sauté lightly until pasta is ready.
Pour mixture over pasta, squeeze some lemon on,
sprinkle with bits of parsley. Salt and pepper lightly.
Eat.

EDIBLE REX

William Burroughs once wrote a fantastically droll satire about a convention of dinosaurs gathered together to discuss the future of their species. The keynote speaker voiced the official dinosaur credo of "bigger is better and biggest is best." As long as they continued to get bigger, the dinosaurs agreed, nothing could stop them.

Today, in an era of Hummers, saline double-Ds, Big Gulps and hormonally enhanced governors, I must admit I feel like I'm sitting in the audience, checking my program, wondering who's speaking after the stegosaurus and whether I have time to get to the bathroom and back.

For you see, in my small world, I am often frustrated by books that teach the basics of vegetable growing. Check that. I'm usually frustrated with <u>any</u> type of gardening book. Why? Because the focus of most of these books is bounty, abundance, the cornucopia; bigger is better and biggest is . . . Hardly ever is there a whisper about quality. Each fruit and vegetable is spritzed with a fine mist of water, lit softly by the rays of a rising sun and artistically photographed at its peak of perfection. Those gardens have never looked as good and they are unlikely to ever clean up as well again. Grandeur! Opulence! Coming to you in Technicolor! More, more, more, more, more. The implication is that if you don't succeed in growing a garden as magnificent and prolific as the ones profiled in the book, well, you should be ashamed—what's wrong with you? Perhaps, you'll be forced by the Chief to hand over your clippers and clogs.

Long ago I worked for a woman who fell victim to the illusions many garden books propagate. She was a garden book junkie with a taste for eye-popping pictures. Nearly every time I visited her home she would greet me in her robe, her hair matted, her eyes rheumy from long hours gazing at her newest collection of garden photos. She'd reverently hold out her latest book to me, opened perhaps to a charming image of calamondins dotting a gravel courtyard situated alongside a priceless view of Lake Como or of espaliered pears clinging to the chinks of a thousand-year-old wall in Prague. Her pasty lips would part and with a dry tongue she would ask me, "Can I have that?" I'd answer with a smile, "Yes. If we're very patient." She'd nod quickly and in a herky-jerky way flip through more pages of beautiful pictures while mumbling, "I want that. I want that." And maybe the saddest aspect of her addiction was that she couldn't see the utter perfection of her own garden. She had spiced roses you could smell from across the street but "not the color I thought they'd be." The continual birdsong her heavily fruited and flowered garden gave stage to was exuberant and awesome and yet, "I hate it that I don't have bigger dahlias." Her vegetable garden was one of my best producing works of art, and while she hardly ever ate any of the goods, she always clamored for "more of those striped tomatoes, they're so beautiful and more of those beans I like, the French ones, the long, thin ones. I want bushels of them. Like this!" And she'd show me a photograph. Poor thing. Hopefully she has found her way into a good twelve-step program by now. If not, maybe you and I can do an intervention.

My humble belief is that if I was to grow a Paul Robeson tomato plant that for some odd reason produced only one fantastic tomato, then it would be well worth the effort. If I merely got one meager bowl of beans from my yard, they would still be far better butter beans than those butter beans Betty buys. (They'd still be alive n' kickin' for one thing. Enzymes and phyto-chemicals that die soon after picking would still be coursing through their little butter bean bodies.) The experience of <u>quality</u> would be mine. I would be tasting the divine. The fresh-picked, perfectly ripe, sun-warmed, slightly bruised, bird-pecked plum is of a quality that cannot be matched by anything store bought. I revel in these experiences. Why worry about being a backyard farmer? Let the farmer be a farmer. The backyard hobbyist's single most important goal should be to grow quality.

Maybe you should forget quantity and remember quality. Especially in your garden. Try it there first. Perhaps it will spill into other parts of your life. Let's not be Jurassic about the whole shootin' match, whaddya say?

"The future will depend on
what we do in the present."

Mahatma Gandhi

WOOD WEEDERS

Increasingly, as I garden, I do less. More often less. Less more often. For as "they" say ("they" being, of course, that completely in-your-face and opinionated Garrison Keillor), less is more. I do less and this is why I do less . . .

In the U.S. today there are more people in prison than there are farming. Fewer than one percent of our population farms, and that number is dwindling even as you read this. And not all the farmers are going to prison; no, surprisingly, hardly any are. Mostly what's occurring is that large corporations like Altria, formerly known as R. J. Reynold's (a truly infamous seller of cigarettes but also the owner of Kraft Foods) are taking over the land and creating giant super farms that we organic health food devotees refer to as factory farms. And the injustice of these factory farms is that they are creating a withered landscape and a citizenry that cannot learn to appreciate nature because nature is being hidden, devalued and destroyed. The farms are of such monstrous proportions that every pesticide or herbicide decision made by the company has attached to it the potential of bringing on ecological ruin. When we had millions of small farms dotting this nation, a single farmer could poison his land without catastrophic effect upon the rest of us. Not so now. All it would take today would be for one factory farm to accidentally spill its supply of liquid beetle killer into the Colorado River to render the waterway basically lifeless.

It's not that corporations are inherently evil. There are people within every corporation who are caring and conscientious. Good people abound. But ethical, well-meaning employees are powerless as long as their company is designed to be an unconquerable market force, a voracious hydra with millions of smacking lips and tentacle-like eyes forever hunting the table for another crumb, another conquest, another turnip to squeeze the blood from. The structure of corporate culture insists that Monsanto is successful only when it dominates, only when it makes large profits for investors. ADM must control its market or perish. Wal-Mart, so large that it accounts for nearly thirty percent of sales volume for companies like Kraft and Nestlé, is generally made up of good folks (Wal-Mart employs roughly one million people) but the corporation itself, by design, is faceless and often, heartless.

If you need an example of faceless corporate avarice, we need only look at the recent removal of diazinon from the marketplace. Diazinon is an organophosphate, a pesticide that was developed by the Nazis in WWII as a prototype for nerve gas. Fantastically, if you have grubs in your bermuda or ants in your pants, you, until recently, could waltz into any old Kmart and purchase yourself a box of nerve gas. Shoot, ain't that the berries? But why was this wonderful poison removed from the shelves, you ask? Well, some people (*weak* people no doubt) get nauseous and dizzy, jittery and dry mouthed, when they play on grass that's had diazinon applied to it. That's what happens to adults. We don't know what happens to kids. We don't measure the effects of poisons on kids. (Oh, by the way, commercial enterprises can still spray apples and green beans and leafy type vegetables with this nerve gas. And diazinon soaks in, it can't be washed away. It's in the flesh. Don't kids eat lots of apples? Hmmm.) Put my two kids together and I outweigh them by one hundred pounds, but they still are exposed to the same amount of toxic residues in apples that I am. They're both around five years old, and their bodies are continuing to develop. I wonder what visits to public parks, to expanses of lawn, these exposures to diazinon are doing to their nervous systems?

Well, other people have gotten worried about these things, too, and enough people were vocal about this issue that diazinon was removed from the marketplace. It will still be sprayed on crops (it's approved for over sixty different crops) and golf courses, but you and I won't be able to buy it over the counter anymore. That is, we won't be able to buy it FOUR YEARS after the mandate was issued. Companies like Ortho and Chevron couldn't just pull their product off the shelf, hell no, that'd be bad for business, they might lose money, no, they needed to sell all the diazinon in their warehouses first. For four extra years children playing t-ball were exposed. The kid with the hopelessly baggy uniform standing in right field and paying more attention to the black squirrel stuffing acorns into the sycamore than he was to the whistling line drive hurtling towards his head, inhaled diazinon unnecessarily as he lay unconscious in the grass. The flower girl, skipping down an aisle of blue fescue, tossing iceberg rose petals into the warm, sun-kissed air—she who so innocently led the spring bride—she was exposed, too. We don't know what diazinon will do to these kids. No, we don't measure the possible effects of pesticides on kids. We play American-roulette with our children's well-being.

But it's a cliché to blame corporations, isn't it? Corporations are us, after all. So, in a way, I'm to blame for these travesties and I feel downright plum awful about it. I could castigate you and the corporations and sit up on my high horse (high on what I've always wondered) but I'd prefer to take some responsibility for this mess of a world and thus, I do less. I do less in the garden because I don't know which corporate product, which newfangled plant food, is going to hurt my kids (or me for that matter). For years I have been using a bagged soil mix, y'know, something you'd buy at the nursery. I've used it, I've recommended it, and I've generally tossed it everywhere without hesitation. And then, recently, I read a public health notice that warned against using oyster shells in the garden. It seems that some oysters have a disproportionate amount of lead in them. Lead is not good for humans to ingest. My favorite soil mix, the soil I've added to many of my vegetable gardens, touts oyster shells as a special added ingredient right there on the face of the bag. True, not all oysters are contaminated and few bags of soil have dangerous levels of lead in them, but the risk is present. Salesmen claim that the lead is found in the flesh of the oyster and not in the shell, therefore, the additive is safe. How do I know? Whom do I believe? I don't. I do less in the garden because I can never be positive that I'm not doing harm to myself and my loved ones.

There's another reason I do less. On a recent trip with my family to June Lake in the High Sierra (an area slated for "development" by yet another corporation), I was struck by an odd revelation. When people walk through the woods do you ever hear them complain of the mess, the lack of proper design? Does anyone ever say they'd like Toulumne Meadows better if it were mown? Does anyone ever look at the fiery trees of Vermont and curse the falling leaves? Do we ever set out on a trek armed with rakes and blowers? Does anyone ever feel the need to weed the woods? Have you ever noticed that there don't seem to be that many weeds in the woods to begin with? Even if you wanted to weed woods you'd be stymied. Because weeds, ironically, are principally manmade. Weeds are nature's pioneers. Wherever land has been cleared and weakened, it is the weed's job to come in and reinvigorate, to take hold, to break up clay, to bind sands, to infiltrate a monoculture and establish diversity. A weed's job is to set the table for trees to grow. Once the woods have been born, the weeds move on to other projects, leaving us to marvel at their masterpieces.

How often when hiking do we point out the gnarled tree? The cedar rended in two by a bolt of lightning, half dead, half living? When we're by a stream don't we kneel down and marvel at the bugs, at the algae, at the ripples of life? When, in nature, do we ever talk of improving it in any way other than discussing how to lessen our impact or how best to preserve it? Don't we all agree that nature is perfect?

Then what's up with our homes? Who taught us to garden like we do? Why all the conformity and redundancy? Why all the manicured and manufactured neatness? Why all the rows, as if the petunias were marching two by two into the Ark? Why do we banish all traces of death? Why are our gardens treated like zoos: specimens set aside and isolated at precisely measured distances from one another, each valued not for its holistic individuality but treated as just another commodity? People don't buy flowers with names, they buy "color." Ask a homeowner how much his garden cost and he can tick off the list of expenses faster than a little boy can behead a Barbie. Ask him how much his garden is worth and he can only reiterate how much it cost and how much it costs to keep it the way it's designed to be. Why do we need to control and limit the garden so absolutely? Are we that frightened?

When travelling on the East Coast, a West Coast lad such as myself is struck by the density of the plant life. Seeing the thick woods on the East Coast I can understand how people of yesteryear felt crushed by nature, how a competitive mind-set was adopted. I can see why someone might have believed that nature was a wild monster born to be yoked. In the past it took enormous energy to keep nature at bay. Control mattered. But today, geez, give me a break. Today nature is whipped. We won. The battle is long over.

In *One Straw Revolution,* Masanobu Fukuoka, a Japanese scientist who worked in the war effort against the U.S., devoted a passage of his book to wild carrots. Carrots are relatives of Queen Anne's lace and have the same profusion of airy flowers when allowed to go to seed. Fukuoka, our former enemy, neglectfully let carrots grow wild in his orchards. After many years of freedom the carrots returned to their roots, so to speak, and began to grow true. When Fukuoka finally pulled some up and ate them he reported that they possessed an earthy and powerful flavor that was thoroughly unlike any commercially grown carrot. The wild carrots seemed much more vibrant to him, lustier, and he was reluctant ever to eat another domesticated carrot again. He consciously allowed his orchards to go "weedy" with carrots from that day forward.

In my small world, I've begun to do what I can to experience such original flavors. My vegetable garden at home is allowed to grow—that's all I ask it to do. I scatter seeds about willy-nilly. I try to throw seeds on the soil in patterns that might occur if they were to fall naturally. I allow my plants to flower and set seed and then I scatter their seeds right back onto the soil much as I imagine it might happen in the wild. I cut off dead parts only to crunch them up and sprinkle them back onto the soil. I plant wherever I find space. I mix it all up. I water irregularly or regularly. I share with the bugs. I get some weeds. I've adopted the idea that if these once wild plants could recapture some of their untamed vigor then maybe, just maybe, I will reap some of the knowledge and insight and taste they once offered.

As a result of doing less, my vegetable garden is beautiful. No business venture could produce it because the garden has no purpose other than to exist. The bounty I harvest from our soil is a gift, a luxury. By doing less, my garden gives me more.

Sandy: "Don't you have to be
      stupid somewhere else?"

Patrick: "Uh, no. Not until four."

SpongeBob SquarePants

WONDERMON

Come with me to the First Methodist Church of God, into the community room/cafeteria/auditorium. There's a big gold-embossed crucifix on the wall, a U.S. flag over there, and a state flag beside it. There's speckled white linoleum on the floor, banks of fluorescents above us. The Teen Scene kids have graced an enormous corkboard by the kitchen with an eight foot poster—"Take a Ride on HIS Thunderbolt, Let Them Hear HIS Thunder!!"

Grab a tray 'cause they're serving fried chicken, mashed potatoes with country gravy, corn and bean succotash, sourdough or pumpernickel, and green Jell-O with cottage cheese and peaches floating in it. Have a pop if you want—oh my God, they have freakin' Tab in the cooler.

Let's sit over here. Well, actually, will you save me a seat?

"Hi, folks, I'm Tony and I'm a Master Vegetablarian." Polite chuckles from the audience. Rule *numero uno,* always start with a joke no matter how unfunny it might be. "I've been asked to join you today to discuss vegetable gardening, edible landscaping and all other matters pertaining to the growing of food. I will be giving two mid-lectures that will comprise half of your letter grade and a final at the end of the lecture that will define the remainder of your grade. If you happen to be in the bathroom while I'm giving either mid-lecture you can arrange to make that up with my T.A.s later in the lecture, but if you miss the final, I'm sorry, there will be no, and I mean zero, make-ups.

"Great, let's start. How many of us are there here? Fifty? Let's say fifty. I'm going to ask some questions of everyone. If you can answer yes to the question, please raise your hand and hold it up until I can count you. Okay.

"How many people here own a telephone? . . . Fifty? Looks like fifty. Good.

"Cell phone? Thirty-two, thirty-three. Thirty-three.

"Television? Right, fifty. Microwave? Forty-two, wow! Personal computer? Forty even. Refrigerator? Fifty. Rice cooker? Fifteen. Okay, okay. That'll do, Pig. We can move on.

"This time please raise your hand only if you are morally, ethically, spiritually, physically, positively, absolutely, undeniably and reliably certain that you know the answer to the question being posed. Here goes . . .

"Who knows how a telephone works? Not 'I pick it up and push the buttons,' but how do it do what it do? Do you know? Who knows? . . . One, er, two. Two of us, maybe three. Good.

"Cell phone? Anybody know how it works? Satellite, yes, but how does that little machine instantly catch the waves beamed up into space and then relay them back down to earth? Over such great distances? Anybody? Yes, oh wow, thirteen. Okay. Now we're hopping. Television? How does the TV work? Remember, be absolutely certain. TV? One. One out of fifty. Microwave? Four. Personal computer? Eighteen of you know how it works. Cool. Fridge? Twenty-five. Rice cooker? How does that little electric pot know how to cook rice perfectly? How does it know exactly, to the nano-second, when the rice is done? Anybody? No, zero. Fifty people. Zero.

"I do have a point. I'm not trying to make anyone feel moronic. As if I could. You'll probably never encounter a life or death situation that will require you to know how a microwave works, much less a big screen TV, in any stretch of anyone's imagination. No, I'm not shouting out your ignorance, I'm exposing a pervasive influence that, I feel, is weakening and diluting our spirits. We live with countless machines that we casually manipulate and utilize every single waking moment of the day and yet we haven't the slightest clue to how they work.

"When everything around you is operating magically, when the complexity of your car engine is too much to learn, when the running of your microwave requires a degree in physics to truly understand, then I find it completely reasonable to expect most people to shut down their inquisitive minds and just let what is, be.

"And sadly, there was a time in the not-so-distant past when a majority of people were quite aware of how things worked and how things were properly assembled. Dresses were made at home from cloth spun and woven by the hearthfire. Chairs made by Shaker woodsmiths are still fine places to rest a big rumbly rump. Those chairs were made to last, made for people who knew how to make chairs themselves. People knew.

"And so, likewise, with our food. When we grew it ourselves, we knew what quality was. Variety. We knew what perfectly ripe meant. We knew that food seldom needed to be adulterated if it was fresh. We didn't need to eat feasts of food at every meal because the vitamin and mineral content of the food we ate was so complete that we were full more quickly. We didn't need to add corn syrup and salt to every food because we were more than satisfied with the authentic version.

"I don't want to disparage the great folks who've cooked for us today, here at the First Methodist Church of God cafeteria. I think they've done a wonderful job of providing, given the palette of food-stuffs available to them. But, please, if you will, look down at your plate. Let's scrutinize our lunches. The chicken was processed—breaded and frozen. The gravy came from a jar I'm assuming. Am I correct?" The hair-netted woman in the back nods. 'Yes,' the judges say, 'yes.' The corn and bean succotash, canned. The rolls were made in a factory with vats of sugars and salts and dextrose, colorings and artificial flavorings all mixed together robotically to create a uniform blob of dough that could be baked and bagged and shipped to market at breakneck pace. The potatoes are instant, the Jell-O is instant, the Tab is not a food, neither is your can of Mr. Pibb. That's lunch, folks. That's what we've set before us.

"And it's not a terrifically bad meal. It's got lean meat, vegetables, carbohydrates, fruit and dairy, and well, uh, it's got Jell-O. But, if all of it were fresh . . .

"People do get on my case, though. They say, 'Oh, sure, wouldn't it be great if we all could have farm-fresh food all the time, but that's just not in the cards. You can't be running around from the orthodontist to the kids' soccer match to the emergency room for stitches and then to the PTA meeting and realistically have honest, healthy food at every meal. It's a nice fantasy, Tony, but it's ridiculously farfetched.'

"You know what I say to that? Bull-oney. We live in a market economy. The truth is that your dollar determines what is available. If you buy only healthy food, convince others to buy only healthy food, soon, very soon, more entrepreneurs will offer healthy food. Every time you buy crap food, you fund the purveyor of crap. Every visit to a fast-food joint gives the burger giants more money to advertise their 'food,' thereby brainwashing others to buy their slop and then, before you know it, the only thing being offered is slop. Stop with the slop. Use your vote. Vote with your money. Vote for better. Better yet, don't vote. Simply grow it yourself and do an end-around past the whole circus of food peddlers and diet deities. Just please do something thoughtful. Please. I need your help.

"Now, yes, let's see, someone had a question about killing slugs?"

Tuscan Slaw

Black Tuscan cabbage (Italian cabbage)
Tangerines
A good blue cheese dressing

Slice up cabbage. Section and slice up tangerines.
Toss with dressing. (Paul Newman's Blue Cheese dressing
is great because, y'know, there's a little bit of Paul in every
bottle, but I always have difficulty finding it in the market.)
Eat.

ABES, RAGS, NUDES AND ELECTRICAL ZIPPERS

I'd imagine you'd like some proof to my claims of being a Master Vegetablarian. "Sure," you say, "he can wax and wane ad nauseam, but what's it worth if all this highfalutin philosophizing isn't being spewed out by a bona fide master of the vegetable? Why should I consider the thoughts of this particular lame-o any more insightful than my next-door neighbor Jim's sound advice?" That's what you're saying and/or thinking. I know. I've been there many a time myself.

First off, let me 'splain you something.

A few years back now, late last century, I found myself sitting in a room with a gaggle of other minor designers staring at a sheet of paper which asked us all sorts of meaningful questions like—model and make of vehicle, cell phone number, name of company, name(s) of assistant(s) etc. etc. There was nothing on the form that struck me as unusual until—PROFESSIONAL AFFILIATIONS: Affiliations? Um, well, uh . . . who?

We sat as invited participants of the Pasadena Showcase House of Design, had, in fact, just walked through the emptied home minutes earlier, and now we were being asked to decide which room in the mansion or which section of the grounds most sparked our interest, and, if we were indeed drawn to a specific area, what genius would we then intend to perform upon said location? I was comfortable being cattle-prodded to respond instinctually, fine with being needled to produce an instant plan, but then, there it was—sneering, mocking, hissing through razor-wire teeth—the question I hadn't seen before, the question I wasn't able to . . . hell, what'n the hell do they mean by <u>that</u>?

I peeked at the paper of the woman next to me. I wasn't cheating per se, but it felt kinda like I was. I peeked at her sheet to see what sort of PROFESSIONAL AFFILIATIONS she had. And she caught me peeking.

"I was, uh, y'know, seein' what uh . . . how're you doin'?"

"Aren't you Exterior?"

She knew I was an "Exterior" designer because I wore steel-toed boots (my good boots I'll have you know) and jeans. I could deduce that she was an "Interior" designer because she was draped in a Helmut Lang black ensemble and wore Matrix-style make-up. Come to think of it, she might actually have been Keanu Reeves pretending to be an interior designer, pretending to be annoyed by my peeking. Keanu or not, her upper lip, painted in the finest postmodern information-age blue that money could buy, curled derisively.

"Yeah . . . yeah, I do vegetable gardens," I sputtered, "I'm gonna do the kitchen garden."

"Are you? How," she searched for the word, " . . . quaint."

We had crossed an invisible line in those first ten seconds that catapulted us into a parallel universe clearly defining us as adversaries. I was now operating in the world of "quaint" and I reckoned there ain't be no harm done if I kept carryin' on like an ignorant rube, so I shouldered right up next to this gal and plunked my calloused and grimy finger smack dab onto her application where it axed, PROFESSIONAL AFFILIATIONS. Behind the colon she had listed: ASID, IIDA, CCID, LOCAL KW40, F.U.D.G.E., M.A.D.D., GLAD, AAA, DMV, and KFC.

"Wow," I said, "you've got a lot of affiliations."

She quickly inhaled and exhaled through her nostrils, effectively blasting me back into my seat.

"Well, yes," the words came coiling, "I wear a lot of hats."

"Ah, lots of hats. That would explain your being macro-cephalic," I said smiling in an eager and earnest way.

"That would what?!"

I paused, looked concerned, "Where?"

"You said some . . . oh never mind. You obviously have no idea who you're talking to."

"Ah-ha! You are Keanu Reeves!!"

She spun and snaked away like a side-winder on a hot interstate. It was the last I ever saw of her.

I got up and moved to a warmer spot in the house, rested my bum on a low-lying window sill next to a guy who, although dressed in a suit and tie, had scuffed knuckles and a bad haircut—"Exterior" all the way. I glanced at his application, and he had scratched a flat line directly after PROFESSIONAL AFFILIATIONS, in essence admitting to the world that he wore no hats at all. I decided, then and there, not to be cowed by such a silly little thing. I smiled to myself and pressed the ink to the paper. MASTER VEGETABLARIAN.

I had completely forgotten about my professional affiliations until a few months later when the program for the event was handed out. Directly beneath my name was listed the title: Master Vegetablarian. And I've been one ever since.

Now, to be a Master Vegetablarian, and don't forget these are my rules, is to be about the equivalent of a yellow belt in Karate. One day I hope to be considered a

DEUS VEGETABLARIAN.

But between here and there I'll need to get my Master Sergeant, Doyen, and Grand Poobah Vegetablarian belts.

As a simple, humble, master of the vegetable, I now ask your permission to share with you some of the tactics I employ in the dirt.

ABES

For about ten bucks you can buy a roll of snail-and-slug-deterring copper tape. Copper, even in the thinnest amounts, captures and conducts electrical current. It is believed that when a snail or slug comes into contact with this copper, it gets "bit" by an electric shock, and hence, in many a garden, this copper tape is used as a low-voltage fencing around precious plantings. The copper tape has a sticky backing and can be applied to the edges of raised beds, flower borders, or on the lips of pots. Unwinding the tape and removing the paper strip from the sticky side is a challenge though. It's akin to, like, well, y'know how when you're wrapping a birthday present for someone you don't particularly like and the tape catches to itself and you try to pull it apart but then you just say "screw it," and you ball up the offensive piece of tape and then peel off some new tape but that sticks to itself, too, and then you wonder in exasperation why you're wasting your time on this idiot and his stupid present anyway!? Multiply that by a power of eleventy and you'll know what working with copper tape is like. First off, it tears — easily — usually in an area you want to remain intact. If you are trying to apply copper tape to a structure or pot that is meant to be artistically displayed, a crooked tear looks way uncool, totally amateur, might as well just start over for all intents and purposes. Or the copper tape creases, causing the same dilemma as a tear. And it sticks to itself better than it does to anything else, but unlike Scotch tape, it's expensive—on my list of unpleasant activities, tossing away fistfuls of copper tape falls right after # 5, Big-Headed Aliens probing me on their mother ship.

So what's a boy to do about snails?

I use these things called pennies. They're made of ninety-seven percent zinc, coated with copper, and they hardly cost anything. They're easy to come by, and they're hard to tear or crease. (In fact, it's against the law to tear or crease them, but that's one of those laws no one really seems to worry about.) When pennies are laid down next to one another they conduct. If you put pennies around your vegetables you are quite literally putting your money where your mouth is. (I'll pause here until your laughter subsides . . .)

Pennies are great fun for the kids. You can tell them that you're paying the snails and slugs to leave your food alone, that, in a way, you're falling victim to spineless extortion. The kids can lay the pennies out flat or they can make the "Great Wall of Lincoln" around the perimeters of each plant. At the end of the season, when that bed is going to be rebuilt, you can have the kids roll up the pennies and keep them. At the beginning of the next season you can get some brand-new, shiny coppers from the teller. Imagine that, you will genuinely go into a bank and talk to someone!

CHOPSTICKS

When you order out for Chinese always ask for a ton of chopsticks but don't eat with them—that's what a fork is for. Instead, use them in the garden. They have many uses. Before they're snapped apart you can push them into the ground "joined end" first and utilize the pressure between the two chops to hold a plant marker, an empty seed package with a picture of the lovely Zulu sunflowers you're growing, or to hold some twine to lay out rows with.

Separated, the chops can be used as tiny stakes for Hungarian peppers that are keeling over. You can stick a chopstick into the ground and make perfect little holes for sowing seeds. You can get down on your knees and use chopsticks for thinning out seedlings. If you're daring or really hungry you can eat the sprouts that you thin right there on the spot. (A note: You will become thin if you thin this way, <u>and</u> if you run miles per day, <u>and</u> if you live on a remote desert island with six other castaways.) If you find that you prefer using chopsticks for eating Egg Foo Yung and Mu Shu Pork at the Poo Ping Palace, very well then . . .

A FORK

can be utilized in many of the same ways as a chopstick can. Forks you'll find in abundance at thrift stores. Forks are a quirky addition to a vegetable garden because they're an obvious design choice but are hardly ever put to use. Forks also can coax out small weeds and are helpful in extracting tomato hornworms from tomato plants as well as for pulling tomato hornworms out of eggplants and putting them back into tomato plants where they belong. (Wait! Don't do that!)

RAGS

The newspaper comes every morning, we open it up, check on the madness, check on the scores, we catch up with Dr. Rex and June, and then we toss the paper into the recycling can (maybe) and send it back to the pulp factory. Instead, I suggest you use the sheets to mulch your beds. The ink on most newspapers is derived from soy and can be considered organic. The shiny color pages, however, need to stay out of the garden because their ink is toxic. Papers are lain atop the weeds and some soil is tossed atop the papers and then the weeds be gone, dontcha know.

Newspaper can also be molded into little planting containers to use for starting seedlings. When the seedlings are big enough you can plant the whole thingamabob right into the ground. You make the holders by wetting some paper, adding a splash or two of soluble glue, like Elmer's, molding the paper around the bottom of a glass tumbler, filling the little paper pot with potting soil and sowing a seed therein. C'est magnifique!

Any good children's craft book will show you how you can make a "newspaper tree." If for some reason your garden is a dismal failure, it's always nice to know that you can quickly "grow" a garden of newspaper trees before your in-laws arrive from out of state.

PAPER TOWELS are great for starting tiny seeds like lettuce. The seeds can be dropped into their own individual paper towel divet at precisely measured distances and will remain in place throughout the watering periods. That is, they won't float away to some other spot. Take a paper towel, preferably an unbleached and recycled towel, lay it on the earth, drop in the seeds, sprinkle *lightly* with soil and water *lightly*. The towel helps to maintain a moist environment as well, but you'll still need to water often to avoid drying out. Here in the West, where we have so little humidity, drying out is a pretty common cause for poor germination.

Another paper towel technique involves bigger seeds—beans. Get out a cookie tray and put it on top of the refrigerator, notice that you haven't seen the top of the fridge in a while— get out the 409 and clean. With your last few remaining paper towels, cover the cookie tray. Take some of your precious rattlesnake beans and put them on the paper towel. Cover your beans with more towels. Wet the paper towels. Keep them moist and in a few days those frijoles will have germinated. Take the tray down, carry the beans ceremoniously out to the garden, and with your chopsticks pick up and place each rattler into its own little peck of earth.

PAPER COFFEE CUP SLEEVES, the kind you'll find at just about every coffee shop, are perfect for protecting new transplants from cutworms, snails, slugs and other crawlers. And because there are more coffee shops in America (I believe the last official tally put it at one coffee shop every forty-seven feet) than there are American insects eating crops, it's a sure bet that you'll have no problem acquiring some of these paper collars.

Wrap them around the base of the transplant, shimmying them into the soil slightly. As they biodegrade the plant will grow and by the time they are dust the plant will be plenty big. Another positive to using this material is that it is customarily a soft brown in color, and so it doesn't have that phony, electric-green-plastic look old soda bottles create when used as protection. The coffee sleeves are much more classy, Dahlink.

NPR

Birds and rodents and kids fluent in Latin are always a problem in the garden, and there are dozens of tricky ways of dealing with each of them.

Birds don't like flashing lights. Where I've got bird problems, I put out a little figurine of John Travolta in his *Saturday Night Fever* pose right there amongst the arugula. If that doesn't work I move up to the mirrored disco balls, mini ones. Next, I hang up promotional CDs. Finally, I flock the entire garden with Christmas tinsel.

Rodents. Good luck. Our only hope of getting the upper hand on rodents is to start eating them. You go first. Of course, there are always cats.

Kids fluent in Latin, as well as birds, and sometimes rodents, can be foiled by imbedding a radio, powered by a small solar disc, into a dried gourd and then using that gourd as the head of a scarecrow. I have found NPR to be quite effective in driving pests out of a garden. Rush Limbaugh and Dr. Laura, I'm sorry to report, suck every living thing out of the garden, good and bad. So, too, does Howard Stern. I have found that the garden responds ambivalently to *Prairie Home Companion* and seems to really like the "Car Guys."

REBAR A GO-GO

I'm kinda known for my use of rebar. It goes back to my early days when I was trying to be clever and thrifty all in the selfsame breath. Rebar (iron, as it is called at the stone and masonry yards) is tremendously versatile. Three-eighths inch rebar can be curled and coiled, bent and boxed in just about any old direction and it can be done by hand. Take a long piece of rebar, find a gnarled fence post or the bumper hitch on that old pickup or the padlock hole on the dumpster behind the golf course or best, the storm drain vents sticking up out of the sidewalk pocked with dozens of perfectly sized holes, insert your rebar and twist, baby. You can corkscrew, zigzag, snake and spiral. Take that art home and stick it in the ground and grow some beans on it—or peas, or grapes, or Malabar spinach, or Armenian cucumbers. Make curly tepees. Make twisty arbors. Make roly-poly trellises. Cheap, fun, disposable. Rebar rules.

And it rusts. Rebar turns a color that is fully acceptable in the garden. Yes, it's metal and man-made, but, in a comforting way, it metaphorically expresses entropy. Everything breaks down and, in this case, the first things to go are things man-made. Rebar gives the garden a sense of age, of decay and ruin, but ironically, it is sturdier and easier to negotiate than bamboo stakes, redwood or any of the other manufactured verticality offered. Look to the iron, youngster, look to the iron.

ELECTRICAL ZIPPERS

Lots of gardens are wrapped in that neon-green stretch tape. You know the look, a classically beautiful champagne grape twirling its way about an arbor, held in place by flapping strips of expanding plastic, the precise color of which came from the bucket-seat upholstery found on a spacecraft now being held within a climate-controlled warehouse in a region of the desert we paranoiacs like to call Area 51. Originally, it is my guess, this garden tape was created for farmers who, caring nothing for aesthetics, wanted a quick tie material that they could easily spot when they wanted to cut something down at the end of the season. That particular hue of green is hard to miss, and it does speed up the process of removal.

I, on the other hand, like to think that I care about aesthetics. I also like things that are practical. Hence, I recommend using electrical zippers. (That's what I call them but they actually go by the silly name, "cable ties.") In your hardware store, hanging there amongst the conduit, union boxes, crimpers and needle-noses, you will find plastic bags containing thin little plastic belts that have a zip catch device at one end. The tip of the little belt is inserted into the "buckle," pulled through and cannot be pulled back—it closes down and holds. Now, electricians use these electrical zippers to bind together lengths of wire inside your walls; me, I use 'em for hanging up tomatoes, melons, cucurbits and kiwis. The great thing about electrical zippers is that they come in all sorts of colors, meaning, you can buy black or white or taupe and voila! the ties disappear within the foliage. They are also easily clipped off when you're done with them. They're recyclable. They're cheap. They're quick. Holy smokes, I'm a fan.

They don't stretch though. Make sure not to tighten them down too snugly, otherwise you may end up garroting a precious vine. No man, take it easy. Give a body some room to breathe when you're fussing with an electrical zipper.

GARDEN GNOME COMPOSTER

When I give a class, I am almost always asked about composting. People seem to think it's an elevated science, an expertise comparable to extracting the DNA from the stomach of a mosquito trapped for millennia in a gob of amber and taking that DNA and growing a velociraptor from it and then, once that dinosaur is big enough, opening a theme park designed to exhibit it. It beats me why folks get so boggled by composting but they do.

Usually, I begin my speech on composting by reminding all those present that everything existing today will be compost in the future. Everything, eventually, turns into something else—recombines. Knowing that everything rots is a good place to step off from because already the process has been intellectually simplified.

"But, but, but . . ." they say. "How d'ya . . . Why d'ya . . . What are them . . . When's a . . . DO I HAFTA . . . ?" On and on the questions tumble out in a panicked flurry. No one wants to believe it's simple; they all want composting to be so mystifying that they won't feel guilty if they don't do it. "Too dang-blasted hard to turn," they'll tell the neighbor, who'll nod knowingly. "Too stinky," they'll tell the dog, who'll wag because he thinks he's being offered a beef stick. "Not enough space," they'll tell themselves while wagging knowingly and chewing on a beef stick. No matter how many times you tell ordinary folks that composting is a no-brainer, they remain unconvinced because the truth is—they just don't want to do it. It isn't sexy. It's down and dirty. It's like changing diapers: necessary but not glamorous. So, I've got this solution.

Take a five-gallon planting can (the black plastic kind that usually come with a plant in it), empty the can, cut off the bottom with a sharp tool (your teeth are not tools), dig a hole in your garden about the size of the bottomless can, put the can in the hole, put a board on top of the can's opening, get a garden gnome or a statue of a peeing cherub, and place this art on the board on the can in the hole in the middle of your garden. You've just built yourself a composter.

Now you can take your kitchen scraps, eggshells, coffee grounds, laundry lint, toe jam etc. and put them in the can. Recover with peeing cherub. When the can is nearly full, dig a new hole, putting the soil from the new hole on top of the stuff in the can. When the new hole is dug, shimmy out the can and put it into its new location. This is a simple, small, and effective way to compost.

If you've got lots of garden waste (leaves, grass clippings, sticks, dead pigeons) you're probably best off making a sit pile for that stuff. Just put it off in the corner of the yard and let it sit. In a year or so it'll be gold.

Sorry. No excuses now.

A SPADE IN THE HOLE

If you come upon a day when you're gardening with someone else, you might want to take the opportunity to transplant a young white sapote or an old Mexican marigold together as a team. Two shovels on opposite sides of a root ball, leveraging up the plant simultaneously, can extract a large plant as quickly and efficiently as a six-year old can pull a wobbly tooth out of her head.

OVA

When transplanting tomatoes I like to provide a slow-release fertilizer that can be found and purchased quite conveniently. I buy chicken eggs in twelve packs— you're probably familiar with them. Into each freshly dug transplant hole I put a raw egg right beside the tomato rootball. I bury the tomato all the way up the stem, leaving two or three baby leaves exposed, and then I water gently, and then I go throw rocks at the pigeons on my house.

Lots of people complain that they grow huge tomato plants but get few fruit. Why? Too much nitrogen. Everybody gets all worked up about gettin' the plants enough nitrogen, and consequently they apply way too much to the soil. Operating under the delusion that "Everything Grows Better With Crap!" we throw bags of poop at every poor defenseless seedling. It isn't necessary. Bigger is not better.

An egg, unbroken, will slowly decompose beside the tomato. As it breaks down it will provide phosphorous and calcium to the plant, both necessary minerals for the production of tomatoes. As it breaks down further it will provide sulphur, which will help the plant fend off disease. Finally, when the plant is well into its cycle of producing fruit, the egg will supply nitrogen, which will then be utilized to create grande tomatoes not mucho leaves and branches.

An egg is cheap, low-tech, in the fridge, and fun.

HEAVY PETTING

It's strange and true that plants like to be petted. A hand run gently through petals and bracts, stems and stalks will utterly thrill your crops. Don't let anyone ever, EVER convince you that gardening isn't dead sexy.

The benefits to petting your plants (and I'm not certain how this works) are a significant reduction in pests, and stouter, stronger plants that produce more veggies. My theory is that lightly running your hand about the plant sends cellular signals that instruct the plant to grow shorter above ground and larger beneath. Root balls are significantly larger after plants are given this attention. As for pests, I think stroking the plants tells aphids and their ilk that the plants might not be a safe haven for reproduction. And I don't think any bug is worried about much of anything except for sex and food and sex and sex, so I suggest you give 'em something to worry about.

NUDES

Droves of ninety-nine-cent stores sell pantyhose at World War II prices (an amazingly low price if you consider that <u>panty</u>hose didn't exist until the late sixties). How? Flaws. As it is with all lines of clothing, there exists a market for seconds. I buy a few bargain pantyhose eggs every year, scissor up the legs into rings, much like calamari, and use them as nearly invisible, super-stretchy bindings for any plant that needs to imitate Houdini. I like to buy "Nude," but they seldom allow me into a ninety-nine-cent store like that, so, typically, I don some threads, grab a shopping basket, purchase some sheer nylons and from there, venture out to my garden.

If it's fertilizer you want, well you can fill a thirty-gallon trash can with water, stuff a single foot of the stockings with a few handfuls of finished compost, tie off the end of the leg (making what looks like a compost kielbasa), drop it into the water, let it sit a couple of days and, presto—compost tea—good for a season.

If you've got snails and slugs nibbling at the shells of your spaghetti squashes and you've just got to have them looking pristine, you can slip a nylon leg over the gourd and let it grow to full size within the protective sleeve.

If you've got a neighbor who always pokes his business into your garden to offer up some unwanted advice and/or to borrow your lawn mower for the thousandth time, there are two effective uses for panty hose that I recommend:

If you are a woman—take pantyhose leg and pull it over your head, slip two oranges inside the nylons, against your face, and negotiate them directly up in front of your eyes. Wait until your neighbor comes out of the back door and then begin to dance about and cackle like a chicken trying to lay an ostrich egg. Having the oranges over your eyes will prevent you from seeing your neighbor's horror and will allow you to commit totally to your performance.

If you're a dude, just take off your shirt and pants, slip on the pantyhose traditional-like, wait 'til your neighbor comes out the back door and begin to dance and cackle like a chicken trying to lay an ostrich egg. Actually, as a man, just try to imagine what it would be like to give birth to anything and then act it out.

Perhaps you hadn't thought of the "Insane Chicken in Pantyhose Trick" before. I offer it to you now, free of charge.

Lastly, if you've got cantaloupes climbing a lattice screen or a trellis you can make pantyhose hammocks for the fruit to rest in as they hang from the vine. It'll look like a party of fat rock climbers bivouacking for the night on the face of El Capitan in Yosemite. Ansel Adams would be awestruck, no doubt about it.

So, there you have it. That's why I'm a master vegetablarian and . . . and . . . that's why.

Okay. Thanks.

"Forty years ago when I came
here there was just a farmhouse and a
small orchard. . . .Bit by bit I
extended and organized it . . .
I dug planted and weeded, and in
the evenings the children
did the watering."

Claude Monet

MAYBE I'LL EAT SOME WORMS

One of my many blessings is that I've been allowed to teach vegetable gardening to elementary school kids once a week. I work for a small private school that has built a pretty cool raised-bed garden smack dab on the asphalt of their playground. My fun is growing unique stuff for the kids so that they'll mature into adults who have seen, smelled, picked and eaten with their own eyes, ears, noses and throats. They get to see one minuscule amaranth seed produce thousands of others. They get to taste foods (like radish pods) that stores don't sell. They get to smell strawberries ripening in the sun. They get to make their own dirt.

I get to learn from them too, of course. I've learned that when you wrap garlic scallions around fresh red-stemmed celery or around a just pulled thumbelina carrot, you are required by law to call it a "garlic taco." I have been reminded that when you're a munchkin you are just as fascinated with dead things (like goldfish floating in the pond) as you are with living things (like goldfish swimming in the pond). I have found that, sadly, the girls labor harder in the garden than the boys—they pull mighty weeds, dig vigorously, heft bags of soil, knock boards back into place, prop plants up—only if and only when the boys are not in the garden, too. If the boys happen to be there the girls do much less work and are far less enthusiastic about the entire enterprise. I'm not sure why this happens and I won't pretend to know. Admittedly, it is only my totally unscientific observation at work here, perhaps not valid at all, but nonetheless, I have learned to give more encouragement and energy towards teaching the girls when the boys are also in the garden. I have also learned that no matter how inured to tales of the strange and offbeat I feel I've become, these kids can still throw me for a wicked loop on occasion.

On hot days I like to spend some of our time in the air-conditioned classroom teaching this, that, and the whatchamacallit of plant life. I try to let the kids talk as much as I am because I feel they spend most of their school day being ordered to clam up. Consequently, *everyone* talks at the same time. But one story silenced us all. There is this boy, nine or ten, beautiful kid, Latino, Italian, Arabic, any of the above. You might call him pre-swarthy. This little guy has eyes that glisten like Omar Sharif's in *Dr. Zhivago* and a bright, infectious laugh. Well, I had been talking about snails and about how the snails here in SoCal aren't indigenous, that they had, supposedly, been brought over from Europe to sell as escargot and that they had somehow escaped. Little Omar started to laugh and naturally I asked, "What?"

"Snails," he sputtered back at me between giggles.

"Snails, what?" I asked intelligently, chuckling myself. In fact, we all were beginning to laugh but we weren't sure why.

Little Omar turned to his buddy, Spanky, and spat out, "'Member, 'member last summer when I . . . when I ate those slugs?"

Spanky began to laugh, "Oh yeah. Seven. You ate seven."

"Wait, wait, wait. What?" I asked in horror, "You ate seven slugs?"

"He did. I was there. I'm proof. Live ones," beamed Spanky. There was a gleam of pride in Omar's eyes as if eating live slugs was markedly better than eating dead ones. And then Spanky and Omar were chortling away again.

They were beside themselves, laughing so hard that they didn't notice the disturbed looks on the faces of their classmates. "'Member, 'member how one of them was crawling back up my throat and, and I could feel it touching the hanging thing in the back and I almost threw up? 'Member?"

"Oh yeah! Hahahahahaha."

"But then I ran and got the hose and we blasted it down my throat?!"

"Oh yeah!! Hahahahahahaha!! "

"So, you didn't throw up and, and you were fine?" I asked again, "You didn't get sick or anything?"

"No, but, but, it was crawling back up my throat!

Hahahahahaha!!! "

Omar thought it so hilarious that I ended up thinking so too. Humorous, though in a different way, was how two weeks later, when the radish pods were perfectly ripe, little Omar refused to try one. He wouldn't give an explanation, he simply refused. Funny what we will and won't do in life. Funny how young we are when we start to develop those boundaries. Funny how that is.

Every few weeks or so I like to eat a bowl full of Foul for breakfast. It's an Armenian dish that is pronounced "fool." It gives me immeasurable pleasure to get up in the morning and dig into some "fool-ishness." It's as easy to prepare as scrambled eggs, toast and orange juice. The main ingredient is fava beans and I am told that "Foul means beans." So there you have it.

"*Beans* for breakfast!? Lord, that must keep you tootin' all day," is the customary response I get from people when I tell them how much I love Foul. They shake their heads disgustedly. In America we eat our beans with supper, dammit. But I figure, what's worse, barking spiders all day or barking spiders all night? Also, if I have Foul in the morn, odds are I'll be outside when the gas man comes a callin'. If I time it properly, Mother Nature will blow some wind right along with me. No harm, no foul.

A challenge for me, though, when I make Foul, is to remember to add cumin. "Cumin is the secret ingredient. You cannot forget your cumin," says Raffi, the friend who gave me the wonderful recipe for Foul. But for some unknown reason, I will have finished eating a bowlful and then think, "Oh shoot, cumin. Idiot!"

Cumin once was the most commonly added spice in European dishes. Romans added it to almost every meal. Slang for a miserly person in Roman times translates into English as "cumin-splitter"— a guy so cheap he'd split cumin seeds (which are pretty tiny) enabling him to stretch out his spice. Cumin was the bomb, man. Cumin rocked. Cumin was major bank. Presently, we have high fructose corn syrup in nearly every processed food, but if we were ruled today by Marcus Licinius Crassus or Caesar Augustus, odds are our most popular flavoring would be cumin. Cumin—the magic ingredient. I won't forget next time I make Foul for myself. I'll just have to get used to using cumin.

Getting used to things is always a task. We humans are always trying to get used to things. We acquire our tastes. Whiskey, cigarettes, Jerry Springer—these things are not naturally pleasurable. People had to become re-accustomed to eating spinach, y'know. At the beginning of the last century, hardly a soul sat down to spinach. Parsnips, that's what you ate. Spinach, blecch! Nobody ate spinach before Popeye came along.

Yes, Popeye. I have a theory that Popeye was on the take from the Spinach Industrial Complex (I also believe that Olive Oyl destroyed the self-esteem of countless young women. I mean, really, how could a girl compete with a body like Olive's?) and now, because of Popeye's shameless promotion, his relentless push push push, we all eat spinach.

Another relative newcomer is the tomato. Tomatoes were originally grown in Europe as ornamentals. Rich royal folk would raise them as annual shrubs with pretty fruits. No one dared to eat tomatoes because they were members of the nightshade family, cousins of belladonna, the poison of choice in those days.

In Thoreau's time people ate the artichoke root, not the flower. Imagine being the first person to eat the artichoke flower, the first Euro to taste the deadly tomato. Imagine being the first goofball to try crawdads. Lobster. Tripe. Habanero pepper. Kefir. Jell-O. ("Here, y'all, I cooked up some horse hoof 'n stuck in some of this here sorghum juice. Taste it ya-self!") When Cortés encountered the Mayans they offered him fudge as a gift. He initially thought it was excrement. I bet the conquistadors lined up for some of that, oh yeah. Imagine being the first to sample a meal of meal worms, cow brains, fried grasshopper, bean curd (anything curdled for that matter), Rocky Mountain oysters, beer-battered scorpion, wheat grass juice, or that green stuff in fruit cake. Imagine those brave, intrepid masticators. What were they thinking?! Were they all just loony? And if they were loony, would you have trusted them when they said, "Mmmm, this is delicious. You wanna try some?" Hell no. It's like the old "the water's fine. It's warm once you get in" trick.

How in the world did all of the foods we eat get to be normal? Will someone explain it to me because I'm truly bamboozled.

You know, maybe I shouldn't have laughed along with little

Omar. Maybe a light should have clicked on in my attic. I should've thought, "I'll own my own slug farm. It'll be big. Huge! I'll have a grand spankin' chain of slug farms." Ha! Then we'd've seen who got the last laugh. Then we'd've been talkin' turkey alright.

But . . . oh, well. Coulda woulda shoulda.

"One of the strange things about
living in the world is that it is
only now and then one is quite
sure one is going to live forever
and ever and ever."

Frances Hodgson Burnett, *The Secret Garden*

A MAP OF THE KNOWN WORLD

The Hanging Gardens of Babylon were once considered one of the Seven Wonders of the World. Those long lost gardens were the only Wonder devoted to a reverence for nature while the other six Wonders were expressions of mankind's desire to dominate nature. Present-day historians struggle to determine what exactly made those ancient gardens built by Nebuchadnezzar so shagariffic, and they may never really know, but, nevertheless, struggle they do. These historians get grants and corporate sponsorships, make documentaries, write papers; they speculate, pontificate and illuminate. But, y'know, there is a far more famous garden that is all too often overlooked, one that deserves serious investigation, a garden that, well, may or may not have existed at all. No matter your belief, I think Eden is a remarkably informative garden to ponder . . .

A garden specially made by God. What would that be like? Would the garden include the forerunner of every species of flora and fauna? Might we find a spankin' brand new gnu or the premiere puma, the newest models to come out of the R&D department? I say, yes we would. We'd have Adam and we'd have Adam ant. We'd have Eve and every other perfectly delectable invention. The earth would be God's creation, but Eden would be filled with His finest and His firstest.

What would you put in your Eden? If you could build an Eden how would you design it? How big, how small? Would you opt for a mountain or Mediterranean climate, or neither nor? Wouldn't everyone's garden, yours, mine and Mister Doodenhopper's, be slightly different in selection of materials? If asked I could go on all day and sometime into the night about my Eden, but here's a thinly sliced version:

Well, first off, we'd need an apple tree, of course. Or do we? Long ago, in the Middle Ages, many people thought the forbidden fruit was a banana. Some folks say it was a pomegranate. A woman named Peg told me just last week that the tree was not an apple but an apricot. Eric once told me that the ancient Aramaic word for "evil" sounded like "apple" when spoken aloud at Mass, hence the confusion. Could that tree, the Tree of Knowledge, which grew fruits possessing the awareness of the concept of good and evil, not have been an apple tree? Hell no, I say. Why should we trust Eric? Or Peg for that matter? Once an apple, always an apple. We can't challenge a belief that's been fed to us over and over for hundreds of years. How dare we think it! Sorry, but Eden gets an apple tree and there'll be no mouthin' off about it, understood?

Okay. And then, we'd have the Tree of Life. It would have to be a magnificent tree, no doubt colossal, with thousands of branches spraying about like fireworks, nearly to the horizon, and it would be protected by a blinding sword of fire spinning in the air in all directions simultaneously. It would be nice to lounge beside the Tree of Life after sunset and thumb through the evening paper by the light of the sword, or in Adam's case (for he had no navel), pick at one's nose and consider the purpose of boogers for a few hours. It would be a bright and cozy spot to spend an evening, a fine place to open up a small café one day. The spinning sword thing might be a little dangerous for the kids to play around, though. We'd have to keep an eye out for that, maybe put a cryptic, small print, freedom from liability clause on the café menu. But, all in all, it'd be it, man, way it.

So, so far we have two trees. What else? If Adam and Eve weren't slaughtering animals for sup, what would they eat? Apples, yes, we've covered that, uhhmm, how about nuts? For protein, nuts would be good—and beans. Yes, we'll need nuts and beans—groves and acres of each—and many different varieties so that they could be harvested all year long. So, we'd have some woods and some fields. And we'd need a meadow, where Eve could pick herbs and spices and seeds and greens for supper, and where Adam could pick flowers to give to Eve in hopes that maybe later that night they could take a tantric roll in the hay. We'd definitely need flowers . . . and chocolate . . . at least a cacao bush so that someday, somewhere, somebody will discover chocolate thereby ensuring the survival of the human race. Okay . . .

1. Tree of Knowledge
2. Tree of Life
   Nuts (walnuts, pecans, almonds, coconuts?)
   Beans (the magical fruit)
   Flowers
   Herbs and spices and seeds and greens
   Cacao bush
   Hay

Now if we're going to have coconuts, then we'll need a lagoon to have a coconut grove. That means a seashore. Good. That means dates and bananas (not forbidden) too. Good. Water!! Positively need water. The garden would have to have a lake with fish and then streams, ponds, waterfalls, bogs, marshes. And a source . . . right, we'll need snow-capped mountains. And we need an arid plain where there'd be some aloe vera to rub onto Adam's rib surgery scar. Okay . . .

   Ocean and/or sea
   Tropical groves
   Meadow
   Lake
   River
   Streams, waterfalls, ponds
   Wetlands
   Mountains
   Arid plain

All of this ideal garden would need to be contained within an area that Adam could walk around in a week or so. Let's say, from dead center (which I think is where we should plant the Tree of Life) it would be twenty miles in any direction to the borders of Eden. That'd make it roughly four-hundred-square miles. That's a decent size garden if you ask me. The fertilizer bill alone would be ridiculous. Oh yeah, this is God's garden, it won't need fertilizing. Good. Within four-hundred-square miles a vast and impressive array of

God's expertise could be utilized.

Outside of Eden, well, you know the story, there'd have to be the Land of Nod. (Have you ever noticed that not one single housing development has ever been named "Nod Estates?") Indeed, God wished us to remain innocent and simple, and like all loving parents, God wanted to give us the best possible world to live in, but, unfortunately, tough luck for us, he planted a tree in the garden that could poison our minds. What a drag. He planted a tree that could infect us with a concept that He probably felt was a mite too complicated for us to deal with, a concept we'd be better off just not knowing about. And then He points at the tree and says, "Okay, I'm going out for a while, leave the damn tree alone," but kids being kids, well— oh, let's drop it. Let's not rehash old dramadies. Anyway, because of that tree we'll need to draw an arrow on the map that points the way to the land of Nod.

In Eden, before that unfortunate family squabble, before we got kicked to the curb for good, there would have existed no pesticides, no fertilizers, no herbicides, no fungicides, no shovels, picks, clippers or hoes (some folks might call Eve a hoe, but not me, no ma'am, not me). There'd never have been any mowing or blowing. No weeding. No pruning. No digging up and dividing. No transplanting with a splash of B-1 to fend off root shock (because there's no use in doing that anyway). Nada. Eden was built the way God thought best.

In the a.m., Adam would have peed outside on account of . . . he was outside. Much like the other animals, he too would not have peed near his water source; he'd have been sure to keep his water clean. At noon, Eve would have picked kale that had also been sampled by a caterpillar. She might not have washed it before eating it. In the p.m., Adam and Eve might have eaten a smattering of vine-dried foods, but most of their meals were absolutely ripe. Dinner would never be boring in Eden; all the foods of the world would be on hand, tens of thousands of them. We all could have supped like Adam and Eve if it weren't for that damn tree. That damned apple/banana/apricot.

One springtime in Colorado, I happened across a small cleft in the hills that was completely socked in with maiden hair fern and sprinkled randomly throughout by thousands of blooming columbines poking their rapturous and gaudy flower faces up through the delicate fronds. This delightful sight totally confirmed for me what shouldn't have needed confirmation at all really—God is the best landscaper I've ever seen. Even if it takes hundreds of years to create a perfect breath of heaven in a nameless gully in Colorado, God's willing to do it. Your God and my God may not have the same name but our God performs the identical magic all over the world and I think, in my odd little way, that we should be students of these designs and techniques and apply what we discover to all of our gardens. They say you can't ever go home again, but I sure think we should try. How would God want your garden to look? How would it look if The Big It did it again? Listen. Observe. Read your map.

"Were they aware that, at least in
thermodynamic terms, the world consisted
of a working partnership between the
sun and the leaf as man looked on –
irrelevant, smiling benignly upon the
scene, secure in the illusion
of his primacy?"

Ian L. McHarg, *Design With Nature*

AN INORDINATE FONDNESS FOR MICROORGANISMS

When Earth came into this universe, she was but a fiery little gasball, a galactic speck born from a supernova's demise. Earth spent most of her first gazillion years as a gurgling, spewing, incontinent mess. She never slept through the night. In those early days, Earth had a smoggy brown atmosphere, soupy brown oceans and land-masses of sleek, dingy-gray granite. Earth probably looked like a big spinning turd. But finally, like most living things, she began to grow into a beauty. Eventually, thanks to primitive molecules that con-sumed carbon dioxide and excreted oxygen, Earth's air grew pale blue, her waters the same. Aeons later, Earth's oceans ceased having steaming hissy fits and began gently to lap at the bedrock of placid lava. Her waters gave molecules of infinite combinations a place to dance, and as devout men of the cloth warn us, the dancing led to intercourse. Complex bacteria sprang forth, both in the water and in the crevices of stones where sediments could settle. These bacteria fed on one another, melded with one another and mutated with one another. And then, gazillions of more years went by. Gazillions, I say.

The bacteria that had become the most successful at being microscopic doodads evolved further. Imagine how boring it must have been to eat the same dang moldy neighbor for an entire life-time. Somebody had to do something! Some bright bacteria had to invent Nouvelle Cuisine. Which is precisely what happened. What they did, ingenious little buggers that they were, was grow their own food. First they grew fungi beneath the pebbles, in the crannies, in the dark recesses, and soon crowded their micro-metropolis to the brink. Then rains came, or winds, ice, or fire, and exposed the back-sides of these fungi to sunlight. A few of these organisms became capable of feeding on sunshine and they soon were sharing this capa-bility with the newest creations on the block—the plants. By sharing, the microorganisms happened upon their most glorious survival mechanism. They encouraged millions of these new-fangled plants to push up through the other bacteria and flourish in the sun. When the plants died they provided a new kind of nourishment for the whole raving party. Other bio-organisms, seeing the success of this enterprise, followed suit. Shortly thereafter, soil and living things sprinkled themselves across the polished granite like a beautiful pox. Baby Edens sprang up in every moist pit, crack and crotch available. Yes, those were itchy days indeed. For much like Machiavellian developers without zoning laws, ferns, lichen, mosses and cycads colluded with ginkgos and pines and eleventy million other ancient plants over an enormous bowl of pasta primavera, and together they joined to quickly cover our Mother Earth. The sun-capturing life fed the underground microorganisms and the micros, in turn, extracted food and minerals from below and fed them to the plants above. Even more progress was made as free-moving life from the seas ambled ashore and began to eat and excrete. Now materials could travel. Those microorganisms hungry for a bit of boron just had to wait for a migrating mastodon to waltz by and supply them with a jumbo pattie. With animals, the soil developed a free-trade system unrivaled as we know it.

Isn't it a clever arrangement? The natural death of one collection of unified cells feeds another collection of unified cells, which, in turn, dies and feeds the other, over and again for as long as the sun continues to shine. How ingenious. How very elegant.

How all of this applies to you is important. As a gardener it is necessary, I believe, to understand and respect your complete physical connection to the soil. Look around you, right where you sit or stand or lie, and realize that all of what you see comes from the soil—even the invisible air that you breathe. Understand that the little critters living in the ground are entirely responsible for your physical existence. You may believe that you have 21 grams of soul that will travel away from this earth one day, but I don't imagine you'd want your decomposed body to go with you. Nope, your skin and its contents are going back to the soil (unless you arrange to have your corpse shot into space). It's typical for us humans to think we're the cat's pajamas here on "our" planet, but if you were a space alien on sabbatical, visiting here to write a scholarly treatise on Earth's living creatures, you might conclude that human beings were more like hair balls than pajamas.

Yesterday, today and far into the foreseeable future, the physical mass of the microorganisms living beneath and within the soil will outweigh the physical mass of all life above the surface of the soil. Take all the lions and tigers and bears, all the beetles, blowfish and boll weevils, take all us bipeds, all the trees, shrubs and kudzu vine— take everything and put it on your great big scale and watch the microorganisms tip the balance in their favor.

We humans then, arguably, are here on earth to serve the soil, to feed the earth, not the other way around. We might just be food for the Gaia. Food for a living planet.

Yes, maybe the earth is a being in her own right: a stellar individual with needs and wants, hopes and dreams. Maybe our Mother Earth likes a good game of cribbage, thinks stardust is scrumpdillyicious, finds comfort in her faith. Who is to say the earth is not a conscious entity? Are the microscopic creatures living on me aware that I, too, am alive? Or do I merely exist as their "heavenly body?" Have they any idea that I live and breathe Laker basketball? Maybe they do, I actually don't know. But my question is this—if, in fact, the earth is "alive," don't you think she wants the parasites that live in abundance upon her to treat her benevolently? At this moment millions of microbes and bacteria are living on and within you. Don't you want them to render unto you the utmost respect? They're living off of you, kid. I think they owe you something.

I have found that when gardeners place their spirits into feeding the soil, the benefits of their labor are immeasurably more beautiful and bountiful. Try it. It may feel right to you. It definitely will feel right to our Mother.

"He is useless on top of the ground;
he ought to be under it,
inspiring the cabbages."

Mark Twain

BRUNFELSIA

Johnny Carson used to poke fun at the city in which the Tonight Show is taped. "Here in beautiful, downtown Burbank," he'd crack, always getting the familiar laugh. To my knowledge, not Johnny, nor Ed, nay, not even Doc ever mentioned the world-famous man the city was named for. Johnny always said, "Jokes about Lincoln will never get a laugh." He probably felt the same was true for Luther Burbank.

I had a conversation some days back with a friend of mine, a horticulturist of considerable knowledge, who had never heard of Luther Burbank. Somehow, although she grew up in Southern California and had actually lived in Burbank, he'd flown under her radar. One of the giants of horticulture, Burbank was responsible for huge leaps forward in the art of hybridization, was the mastermind behind numerous new strains of crops and led Los Angeles County, in his day, to become the number one producing agricultural region of the world. Luther Burbank made Burbank what it is. Burbank! My friend's lack of Luther knowledge is tantamount to an actor not knowing who the Lunts were, an electrician never having heard of Tesla. It's comparable to a Roto-Rooter guy not knowing who John Crappe was.

Crappe invented the toilet. He named his invention the "Crapper." I wonder every so often if Crappe's descendants are proud of their great-granddad as they sit on a cold seat on a frosty morn while outside the door other family members stomp and cry out desperately, "C'mon! What're you doing? Writing a novel?!" Crappe the Elder's invention changed the world. Again, I wonder if any of the offspring Crappe left behind think much about johns. After all, the world keeps a spinnin' and spinnin'. It would be easy to take commodes for granted.

I mean, you've heard of Shakespeare, maybe even read some of his stuff, but have you read Ben Johnson? Ben was pretty hot in his day. If Shakespeare is the greatest writer in the English language, Hugo in French, Cervantes in Spanish, who's the best in Chinese? Do you know? Who's the best Indian actor the world has ever known? The best dancer to hail from Auckland? Who's the master fisherman of all time? Who's the world champion bowler right now? Top rodeo clown? Finest needlepointer? Best craps shooter? Of the Crappe family, who's the best craps shootin' Crappe?

Four hundred years from now people will probably still listen to the Beatles. Folks will picnic "on the green" for performances of BeatleMania. It will, unarguably, be an exceptionally gentile under-taking. On the other hand, in the future, I don't think people will be listening to The Archies, Slim Whitman, or Milli Vanilli (no offense, y'all). Four hundred years from now people will definitely be watching reruns of Gilligan's Island and the Brady Bunch (I mean, duh), and it is likely that the nation of Lilbuddia will require each of its citizens to wear white cotton pants, a red, long-sleeved shirt and floppy sailor's cap while overseeing official government business, but do you, even for a second, think anyone will give a hoot about "who shot J.R." or "who killed Laura Palmer" or "who wants to marry my Dad?" Heck no.

Tell me, what did your great-great grandfather do for a living? You have eight great-great granddads to choose from. How did one of 'em bring home the bacon? One of my great-great granddads made pickles. He was a professional pickler. I think. It might have been my great-uncle who was the pro pickler, covering the circuit, dealing with the fans, the gherkin groupies, the pickle paparazzi. Maybe it wasn't my great-great granddad at all. Geez, I dunno. That man might have saved, for all of us, a rare German cucurbit. He might be my greatest hero. I just don't know. How embarrassing. Maybe some ginkgo will help my memory.

Ginkgos are the last remaining member of their family. Orphaned by time, ginkgo trees have been around since dinosaur dung was the most common fertilizer. But then, obviously, plants of all kinds have been present since the dawn of man. They preceded us and will likely outlast us as well. Plants are as thorough and inform-ative a web-work of connective tissue to the past and future as any library of books. They are natural historians. Some bristle cone pines living and growing today were seedlings when Jesus taught. I believe their story of perseverance, tolerance and adaptation is a good one, too. Legend holds that potatoes pirated from the belly of a Spanish galleon as it returned from South America were brought to Kent by Sir Walter Raleigh where they transformed the Irish food supply, allowed the Industrial Revolution the workers it needed, later forced famished Irish emigrants to U.S. shores, which, in turn, resulted in Marilyn Monroe singing, "Happy birthday, Mr. President." Without the potato in Ireland (oh, I do shudder in me very bones to think on it, Lass) the world might never have been given sour cream Lays.

How will I be remembered in the future? Not for my pickles, that I can assure you. Eventually, not a solitary soul will have knowledge of my prior existence. But if not my pickles, well then the plants I pass on, the seeds of those plants, the foods they produce, that's how I'll stick to the ribs of the generations to come. My work with heirloom plants will, in its own way, have as profound an effect on humanity as Michelangelo's Sistine Chapel. So could yours. Barring a future cataclysmic disaster, our efforts today in our modest little vegetable gardens, tending antique vegetables and herbs from lands and times long departed, will help feed the mop-headed kid having her first picnic "on the green" while she twists and shouts to the four-hundred-year-old tunes written by those fabulous lads from Liverpool. Bon appétit, ma belle, bon appétit.

"And then Sven looks over at Oli
and says to him, 'No, Oli.
It's a bit, you know, sexier if the
potato is in the front of your
swim trunks, not in the back.'"

Uncle Dave

OFFAL AIN'T
ALWAYS AWFUL

One of the benefits of our modern world is the abundance of waste. There is so much excellent garbage out there just free for the taking that I'm never at a loss for compost materials. I can drive around and in less than an hour, fill the back of my pickup with a cornucopia of draff. Here are a few sources to consider.

1. Many fast-food joints, as well as Mom and Pop coffee shops, pre-crack hundreds of eggs and mix them into buckets so they can ladle them onto the grill in a quick, efficient and Orwellian manner. They bust the ova early in the morning and usually fill a thirty-gallon trash bag with the shells, and that's a lot of calcium and phosphorous to be had. (Note: big franchises, like MickeyD's have their eggs shipped in pre-mixed, undoubtedly in an effort to create less on-site trash [hurray!], but, just as likely, because the McSuit's would rather be dipped into special sauce before they'd give, god forbid, <u>anything</u> away for free [hiss!].) If you do collect eggs, be sure to wash your hands and other free-swinging appendages after adding them to your compost. The heat of the compost pile should cook the bad critters on those shells, so you need not worry about that. Sometimes the bags of shells will have other trash to sift through but usually it's coffee filters and grounds and hey, you can compost those too, because –

2. Starbucks and probably other coffee shops give away their trash bags filled with used espresso grounds. The grounds are great for your grounds. They are sterilized by the espresso machine so they add only a little nitrogen in the way of nutrition, but they do add ample acidity (in the West we have alkaline soils so upping the acidity is usually a good thing to do,) and they also add texture to the soil. Coffee grounds will also stain your soil darker so that it seems healthier, which improves a gardener's enthusiasm, which makes you want to garden more . . . and more and more and then go get more free, free, FREE coffee grounds and garden more 'n more 'n more and get more grounds, gotta get more coffee and then, then . . . Huh? Oh. Sorry.

3. Jamba Juice and other fruit smoothie joints go through cases of oranges, and yessiree, those orange rinds go into their own bag and into the dumpster. But don't dive into the dumpster, that's only for <u>professional</u> street people. Rather, visit these places about ten a.m. or two p.m., basically right after their rush periods, and ask for the orange peels. In my experience, they are more than willing to let you drag that jumbo bag out of their store.

4. Hair salons, barbershops, and best of all, pet-grooming places have plenty of hair to spare. Hair has loads of micronutrients and minerals in it and breaks down completely in the compost pile.

5. Grocery stores throw out old produce every day.

6. Garden centers throw out old plants every day.

7. And the big daddy of them all, if you're looking to mulch a large area, is to find a tree-trimming company and ask them to come unload an honest day's work on you. Arborists are often willing to take a side trip, a scenic tour, if it also includes avoiding the payment of dump-site fees.

Trees possess minerals from way down deep, micronutrients that aren't always available in other soil mixes. As they decompose, tree trimmings do wonders to promote the growth of healthier soils.

Recently, I've heard tell of a guy who consciously defies the "Laws of Land" by using truckloads of sawdust from a door-making company to create his compost. He mixes the sawdust with a mountain of horse manure (there's some thrashin' snow boardin' on the north face, hombre). I think the heavy amounts of nitrogen in the manure balance out the sawdust's nitrogen-leaching effect. He also collects sweepings from the street-cleaning trucks. Against common logic, this guy has superb compost and a spectacularly successful garden. And he gets it for free.

So just think, in a short time, you too can become a bonafide and certified garbage picker. Won't your parents be proud?

"In the wet months, blackberries
        spread so wildly, so rapidly that dogs
and small children were sometimes
        engulfed and never heard from again.
In the peak of the season, even adults
        dared not go berry picking without a
                military escort. Blackberry vines
pushed up through solid concrete,
        forced their way into polite society,
                entwined the legs of virgins,
        and tried to loop themselves over
                        passing clouds."

Tom Robbins, *Still Life With Woodpecker*

WILD THING, YOU MAKE MY THING SPRING

Just over seven thousand years ago, on June eleventh, our shrewd ancestors decided to quit scrapping for food. Today, in this hustle-bustle world, we chase the almighty dollar; back then, they chased the almighty buck (the one with a rack on top). All that zipping around must have been a big pain in the arse, because one particular old curmudgeon, a guy by the name of Boyle, suggested to the people that they put down roots somewhere about the river Jordan. And so it was.

Anthropologists have taught us that the first crops cultivated were grains, ancient wheats. Not surprisingly, these maiden experiments in organized farming grew grains, as often as not, for the purpose of making beer, a Mesopotamian beer named Boozo. Of course, once they began drinking beer, they wanted pretzels. That's how people learned to make bread—from a pretzel craving. See how simple history is?

Next, the elders looked around at all the weeds and wondered, "Hmm, why is it weeds grow so well? Man alive, I wish we had ourselves a machine that could transport messages across the ether so we could ask old Pilar about them weeds." Admirably, rather than sit by and wait for Al G. Bell to come along, the elders got busy. Trusting their gut feelings, our foremothers collected the seeds from these weeds, renamed them "greens," and began to cultivate them along with other promising plants. Soon thereafter, people could have peas porridge hot with their pretzels and beer. Later on, they would look to the trees and ponder sticking that pecan nut into the ground a way abouts over there. They sowed it, and it grew. Thanks to them, you and I can wolf down butter pecan ice cream so quickly that we get brain-freeze.

The original plants chosen for agriculture were selected for their strength and reliability. Of the thousands and thousands of edible plants available, our predecessors chose a specific few and indelibly changed the world. They began hybridizing, grafting, forcing, training, saving, cataloging and documenting all of the plants they had chosen. Today, our supermarkets are a reflection of the diligent selections Boyle and the other people who lived thousands of years ago decided upon. The worldwide menu has changed but a smidgen from then to now.

Gazing at a tomato vine last summer I realized that the plant, left to its own devices, would grow like devil grass; it would send out runners and eventually an entire web of tomato would thrive. A tomato is a tropical plant and in the frostless tropics could probably be grown as a perennial. (Here in L.A., I usually harvest my final tomatoes in January, pull out the plants which will sometimes still have green fruit on them, wait till March first and start tomatoes directly in the ground again.) The tomato vine allowed to lie on the ground sets out roots along the stem where it comes in direct contact with the soil. If the mother plant dies back the other rooted areas can continue to shine on. But today, in our traditional backyard farm, using techniques passed down to us from our Boozo-drinkin' ancestors, we cage up our tomatoes so as to keep the fruit off of the ground, high above any pesky soil-born diseases. We cage them up and tie them to their bars. A number of us wicked gardeners even pinch their crotches to keep the libidinous, self-pollinating tomato from erecting suckers. We do our damndest to keep the tomato in bounds. Yet it seems to me, if a tomato had its druthers, it'd be fancy-free, emancipated, at large to roam the countryside.

And so I began to ask this question about all of the foods we know and love—what were they like in the wild? They were all wild once—how did they thrive? What made them stronger than the other plants, what made them reliable enough to be chosen by people who had previously existed as hunters and gatherers for a thousand or more centuries? How much egg could an eggplant plant if an eggplant could plant egg?

When we overseed our lawns, we freely cast a bucket of winter rye over an expanse, top it with some manure-enriched soil, and water it in. The grass usually comes up uniformly and lushly. When we plant carrots, whose seeds are smaller than winter rye seeds, we should sow thickly, too. I like to mix radish seeds with carrot seeds because the radishes grow twice as fast, and the simple task of harvesting radishes also thins the carrot crop sufficiently. But when carrots are left on their own to flower and seed, the "birthrate" of new carrots is remarkably different from when densely planted by humans. First, the number of seeds produced by a single carrot would fill five or six seed packets; the odds of reproduction are of paramount importance to the mother root. (The mullein plant can produce up to four hundred <u>thousand</u> seeds!! <u>per</u> flower head.) Secondly, the carrot flower, like its relative, Queen Anne's lace, stands high and reaches away from the mother root. The seeds are meant to fall a distance away, perhaps to be scattered by autumn winds. As a consequence, carrots self-seed quite haphazardly. When a seed leaves home for parts unknown, it will almost always bed down in a snug nook between rotting leaves or at the base of an accommodating cabbage or rutabaga. I have found that seeds allowed to plant themselves gravitate to other warm bodies, towards other established plants. Given protection, these are the carrots that typically do the best. On a farm you'll see hundreds of carrots in a row, carrots and only carrots, a monoculture, but that is not what the carrot is hardwired to do. Better to see hundreds of carrots in amongst hundreds of lettuces, in amongst dozens of peas and beans, amongst peppers and parsnips . . . those are happy carrots. Those are wild carrots.

Peas have tendrils. Why did they evolve this way? So they could attach themselves to other plants, right? They grow in cooler weather, so typically a pea plant catching a ride on a winter-defoliated shrub will have grown to a substantial size before the shrub sets out its new leaves. By the time the summer heat starts kicking in the leaves of the shrub will help shade the pea plant from too much sun, and the precious pea pods will dangle inside the shrub, protected. Think about it, peas evolved without mankind. We were not part of the Pea Equation. Peas, using their pea brains, came up with this plan of action all on their own. And lest you think this undertaking only benefits the pea, don't forget that the pea sets nitrogen into the soil. The pea fertilizes the shrub. The pea season is finished, the pea vine withered and done long before the shrub needs to set its own fruit. In this design, both pea and shrub benefit. Nature, I have decided, always tries to play fair.

Recently, while reading Henry David Thoreau's "Wild Fruits," I was totally struck dumber to find that the Ancients listed grapes as trees. If I understand the text correctly, grape vines grew so immense as they wound their way up trees that if the tree died it was common for the grape to remain standing on its own. We're not talking about small trees either. Thoreau would suggest that the trunks of these grapes were so large that artisans carved statues of the deity Jupiter from them (Jupiter, by Jove!). Not only were the plants physically impressive, the mere process of harvesting grapes in Thoreau's time was equally daunting when you consider, "eyeing the big purple clusters high on the trees, and climbing to them—shinning up a vine as a sailor a rope." The vines were as thick and long as ship ropes? Have you ever seen a grape like that? My mother's house in Louisiana has muscadine grapes growing wild in the trees and I've tried climbing those vines—and nearly broke my blame fool neck. Ain't no sailor's ropes there, no sir. I cannot for the life of me imagine climbing vines for a living. One hundred forty years ago in New England it may have been a common sight to see some poor schmuck swinging through the trees.

By looking for the wild side I've stumbled upon other truisms particular to SoCal. For instance, it took me years to realize that peppers in this Mediterranean climate I live in can be considered perennials. Until this year I dutifully yanked 'em out every fall. Duh.

Potatoes sown within a hodgepodge of other vegetables three years ago are still producing nicely. Every so often I'll rummage through the soil and drag out a couple of lunkers.

Italian black cabbage just continues to set out side stalks month after month with no sign of stopping. If I had harvested the whole thing, I might never have known it could do this. The cabbage is going wild, and I love it.

My chard plants grow to eight-feet tall before the weight of the flower head drags the stalk to the ground. Where the stalk hits dozens of infant chard burst forth.

I have golden beets in one garden that are two and one half

years old. Most of the roots are woody and sit on top of the soil, but the greens (actually they're golden/green) are still quite delectable.

Cucumbers have never self-seeded for me, and I've yet to figure out why (cucumbers are originally desert plants, they should be sprouting up all over the dang place)—but I'm looking forward to the day when I can eat a savage cucumber.

Squash needs no encouragement to spread its seed. I don't think we've ever really gotten the upper hand with squash. Maybe we should go out and kick some zucchini butt, what d'ya say?

My gardens are getting wilder and more spirited with each new season. To my way of thinking they are much more appetizing simply because of the adventures they are beginning to offer. There will always be a safe familiarity to vegetable gardens but there will also be many surprises. How cool.

Speaking of cool, I know most of us in the U.S. of A. live in climates that are much chillier than here in Los Angeles, but you in the snow also have springtimes that bring a walloping flurry of life, and I'm sure that within that window of time there exist opportunities for you to see what might happen if your garden were allowed to go wild. You in the cold, you probably have remarkable discoveries awaiting you. Heck, Thoreau filled volumes with his waxings on the merits of wild plants. It was cold sometimes at Walden Pond, wasn't it?

Left on its own would the radicchio reincarnate? Would the beans burst and bring forth new generations? Would chaos ensue or would nothing significant happen at all? Who knows? Only you can find out. My point, finally, is maybe more of us should be like Boyle, stop chasing the buck and start experimenting with something different.

"Calculating Irrigation Needs

Stark and Miller developed an equation that shows the enclosure influence or skyview on the net heat load:

Net heat load, cal/min = $-1463 + 3574 Vf_{syn}$

where Vf_{syn} is the synthetic view factor, or the decimal proportion of the skyview comprised of synthetic (buildings, etc.) materials. They find that the heat loading becomes positive when Vf_{syn} exceeds 0.41. A tree located at curbside in front of a building on a city street may have a skyview of at least 0.50 or greater.

To eventually calculate irrigation rates, the heat loading must be applied to an evapotranspiration equation based on the heat budget."

Phillip J. Craul, *Urban Soil in Landscape Design*

(Tony's note: it is a good idea to water when things seem dry)

THERE'S BOOTY BELOW

Several years ago I discovered, quite accidentally, that many early cultures around the world grew their crops in sunken garden beds. By sunken, I mean, more or less, the direct opposite design of a raised bed. Instead of boards boxing in the soil, you have boards boxing out the soil. The indigenous people of the Southwestern U.S., the ancient Egyptians, Syrians, Persians and, I'm guessing, other hot and bothered farmers along the agrarian timeline, adopted this practice for logical reasons—it works. I mean, these people had to survive on their agricultural know-how. There wasn't a market to run down to. Harry and David weren't mailing pears and avocados. No, these sun-soaked folks needed to sustain themselves and the sunken vegetable garden was the solution they came up with. This little discovery made me sit up and rub the sleep from my peepers. I had to try it.

Let's see now, what exactly is the purpose of a raised bed? Well, in Fargo, ND, where the soil freezes impregnably (only to be exceeded in density by my Dad's old concrete toenails), a bit of raised dirt warms quicker in springtime than your regular ground-level dirt. A raised bed allows you to lay out your Chiogga beets sooner and/or drill some sweet corn weeks before the local farmer is able to break out the plow. (A side bar, if you please . . . Having been raised in SoCal, it had never occurred to me until recently, that if you happen to die in January in Maine or Wisconsin or Alberta, they can't plant you into the ground until spring thaw. Somehow, the thought of all those bodies stacking up in an icy cinderblock morgue, a corpulent, pale, hockey-crazed goon watching over the popsicle dead, kinda creeps me out. It'd probably make a decent setting for a horror film, and, y'know, you can have that idea if you want. I mean, I don't like horror films. If you want to use a wintry dead house as the background of your next blockbuster, feel free. Have at it. More power to you.) To be brief, which, it would seem, is impossible for me to be, a raised bed gives you a jump start.

Now, think about a woman in Vegas. Not that one. Think about the mother of four who wants her kids to eat some . . . any vegetable and takes up the idea that she is going to plant her brood an edible garden. Does she need to warm her soil early? Even though it's ninety-five on Valentine's Day, should she strive to get that soil up to an even one hundred? Obviously not. But, poor dear, if she were to pick up 99 percent of all the literature out there and look for instructions on how best to plant her vegetable garden, she'd think the proper way, nay, the only way, was to build raised beds when, in fact, she'd be far better off submerging her garden. By lowering the soil about a foot you gain many advantages in the dry, hot West. First, water doesn't run off, it pools up. You can flood the whole bed if you want, and because water flows to the lowest point, all other ambient watering in your yard will seep into the veggie beds if they are situated properly. Second, if you plant densely you can create a microenvironment, a shade canopy, much faster in a sunken bed, thereby, again, helping to conserve water while maintaining plant vitality. Thirdly, a sunken bed just stays cooler, and that's certainly helpful in summer when weeks of quadruple digit temperatures can be the norm. (As I write this today, July 23, here in L.A. it is 1,007 degrees. With the heat index, it feels like, I kid you not, at least 1,019.)

To construct the beds, you first mark out your space (longer and thinner is better than shorter and wider). You can make sunken garden beds rectangular or winding, kidney-shaped or pancreas-shaped, whatever you want, just be ready for some digging. I recommend digging down about two feet and piling the dirt just outside the perimeter of your design. If the soil is cement-like adobe, then you'd be advised to soak the area overnight to soften the clay. Even after soaking you may only be able to get down one shovel-blade length. Dig out what you can and soak it with water again. And dig again. Eventually, the piled soil will raise the inner edges of your bed and ultimately give you more depth. After you've dug out the bed go have yourself a Swedish massage or a Swedish meatball and then, mentally prepare yourself for more digging.

Next get some good organic materials: compost, gypsum, a dash of manure, some earthworm castings, and shovel them into the hole. Add enough good stuff to raise the soil back up to about a twelve-inch depth. I suggest you lightly blend the new stuff into the old soil, beginning at one end of the bed and working your way out backwards so that you don't compress already enriched soil with your nasty old clodhoppers. Now, from the inner rim, you can line the walls of your veggie garden with stones or bricks or boards, just so long as you have something in place to retain the soil. If you've made the bed narrow enough you shouldn't have any trouble reaching plants from either side of the trench. After all that is done, flood it. A half-inch of water will do. Time how long it takes to drain. If it takes over thirty minutes, you may want to push holes deeper into the soil and fill them with pea gravel or more gypsum so that you won't end up with a poorly designed pond in your back yard. Finally, plant away.

When your plants are small, it is easy to cover the beds with shade cloth or fine-woven row covers simply by stretching out the material and anchoring it with a heavy, blunt object. (Warning: although large enough to hold down shade cloth, cans of baked beans with honey smoked ham will explode! if left out in the hot sun. Nothing like pulling bean shrapnel out of your bum to ruin a perfectly fine afternoon.) Shade cloth will not only give your seedlings a more favorable light, it will also slow down marauders who might feast on your babies.

Naturally, all new constructions need some tinkering and each new garden has its own set of rules, but I strongly urge you to experiment with this style, especially if you live west of the Rockies and don't get much, if any, summer rain.

"There is a mountain in Germany, called the Brocken, nearly a mile high, where a man's shadow is sometimes thrown on the clouds."

Book of Wonders and Curious Things

WHAT IS OF ESSENCE . . .

Consider the wee atom. Bunches of puny electrons spinning about a central nucleus which contains, tinier yet, protons and neutrons. Did you know (you probably did) that within the atom there is more space than matter? There is more nothing than something in these guys. There is proportionally more space in an atom than there is in outer space. Now think about what is made up of atoms—EVERYTHING! Every single thing consists of atoms. You and me and that chair and that window and that splat of pigeon poop (%&!#@*-ing pigeons!!)—all of it atoms. All of it space, or, mostly space. Oranges and apples—mostly space. The dirt under your nails—mostly space. If the maxim for a retail business is "location, location, location," then the truth of physical reality is "space, space, space." If a lover ever again says to you, "I just want some space," you might want to point out to them that they already consist of plenty of space (especially do this if you want the relationship to be over, dead and done with in the immediate future).

Which leads me to this—what is this space, this nothingness? Is it God? Will we ever know? Can this space, which exists more abundantly than anything else in the universe, interact with the space held within my cells? Can your space affect my space? Personally, I sense that it can and does. I doubt that it can be scientifically proven at any time soon, but on a gut level, I feel that the pure space within us flows . . . like water . . . like a breeze . . . like love. My own truth tells me that space is hardly empty, no, not in the slightest degree. Rather, I perceive space, our space, to be the whispered breath of God.

In the past several years, physicists have been unraveling the mysteries of the universe using a whole slew of whiz-bang theorems. One hypothesis that speaks to me is string theory. String theory is all mathematics and thus resides in a language that is difficult for me to understand thoroughly—it swims around my perimeters. Therefore, as a gardener I'll learn the basic buzz of plants, soil and light thank you very much and kindly allow the folks at Caltech to do what they're good at—math. What I can fully appreciate is what string theory tries to do. String theory attempts to blend the laws of thermodynamics (which explain atomic workings) with the laws of general relativity (Einstein's work). Both immensely large and minutely small entities can be viewed and dissected using string theory (or so I'm told. I mean, they could tell me anything and I'd have to believe them, right? "String theory, huh? Sounds good to me. Keep at it, Poinsy. No, you can't modify my Gameboy for me, thanks.")

One of the more fascinating notions to come out of string theory is the idea that there are at least eleven, count 'em, ELEVEN dimensions of physical reality. Some scientists are now saying there may be as many as twenty-two dimensions. I say, let's stick with eleven because, I don't know about you, but I can only experience three dimensions any way I look at it. Maybe I'll learn to experience more dimensions in my enlightened future, but for the time being I'm stuck at a paltry three. That leaves eight more dimensions spinning pell-mell about me, all dancing in an invisible cosmic soup that I can't even begin to appreciate. These other eight dimensions have influence on everything around me, and I haven't the slightest clue as to what they're doing. These invisible eight could be making my trousers too snug—at the knees. They could be forcing me to use the word "trousers" in that last sentence, who knows? They could be making the Pontiac in front of me go way too slow while the Plymouth behind me goes way too fast. The invisible eight could be conducting all types of practical jokes that I'd never see, never know to laugh at. Eight other dimensions—man, that's a whole lot of nothing goin' on.

One visible, and hence, comforting dimension of life is light. In fact, without light there is nothing to see. Light falls on just about everything here on earth and just about everything here on earth needs light to survive. We humans, we can only see a fraction of the light. The largest portion of light doled out by the sun is infrared. We don't see it. Dogs do to a degree. Cats. Owls. Giant Squid. Ricky Nixon was rumored to have seen infrared, but like dogs, only to a degree. Ricky's primary sense organ was his nose (again, a rumor).

And then, of course, at the other end of the spectrum is ultraviolet. There's not much ultraviolet to see but it doesn't make any difference because we don't see that either. Bugs <u>do</u> see ultraviolet though. Some rather dull flowers (to our way of thinking, that is) are striped with runways of ultraviolet. Like neon signs flashing "vacancy, free HBO" or "Gretzky Shoots—Jesus Saves!" these flowers advertise with ultraviolet gaudiness, and unless you and I put on special gizmo lenses, we'd never know it.

Some single-celled organisms aren't capable of filtering out any of the light spectrum so that, sadly enough, they're the only living things on earth experiencing all of the light waves the sun is emitting. I wonder how many dimensions they can participate in, these paramecia. Five? Six? No, probably only one. Nature's like that. "Okay, Squirmy, I'm gonna let you experience all the light. That's the good news. Bad news is, you're not going to genuinely see anything, and, in fact, you'll only be able to experience one single dimension. You'll kinda be like the politically correct blind character on a mid-season replacement sitcom. Sorry, chum, it's the best we can do."

Antoine de Saint-Exupéry's character, the Little Prince, discovered perhaps the most important truth. He learned, "What is of essence is invisible to the eye." I often think of the Little Prince and his lesson. When I work in the garden and an invisible breeze flits past me or the invisible scent of lilac drifts into the holes in my head or when invisible gravity makes the drizzle fall, I try to remind myself to thank what I cannot see. I wish the invisible a good day, hope you're doing well, some kinda weather we're having, that sort of thing. And in cherished moments I can sense that even though there is more at play here than I will ever be able to witness or understand, it is simply my blind, three-dimensional existence that makes everything worthwhile. We are here. We are here to take note of it all. We are perfectly here with everything else and the interactions between us all transpire flawlessly in an endless wash of space. I have been taught by the invisible that my vegetables are more God than food. That I am filled with more God than gardener. As are you, buddy, as are you.

Gardens can give us far more than physical sustenance. They can feed our souls.

Make the revolution attractive.

DEAD BUG WALKING

I am asked every blessed day how best to kill something. Invariably, each and every time that I speak to someone about gardening, I will be asked, "How do I get rid of . . . Snails . . . Aphids . . . Moles . . . Gophers . . . Rabbits . . . Giant Whiteflies . . . Dwarf Whiteflies . . . Giant Farting Husbands?" Etcetera, etcetera.

HOW TO KILL
Fail-proof Ways to Expunge Every Icky Living Thing from Your Garden!

would probably be the best-selling gardening book of all time. People, it seems, are fanatical about committing murder, especially if they don't run the risk of being put into a prison cell with a large imbecile named Horst for twenty to life. Folks can really get behind a good day of carnage if there's no punishment involved.

Gardeners often ask me what do I do and well, if I'm in a mood, I'll simply answer, "I don't kill (fill in the blank)," and then I smile. "No, seriously," is the usual response from the serious exterminator. If I further champion the idea that killing is unnecessary, I am witness to a full retreat. People cannot tolerate the idea that annihilation is unnecessary. They physically shut me out when I tell them that. You can almost see their ears curling in on themselves so as to muffle the offensive noise. If they too happen to be in a mood that day they will sometimes rebut with, "But killing is natural. Nature kills all of the time. A hawk feels no remorse. A scorpion is a scorpion. Why should we be any different?" To which I say . . .

If you need to kill, then kill like nature kills. Nature kills proportionately. Nature seeks balance. I urge folks to, if they must rub out creatures infesting their plants, do it by hand. That is the natural way. No tools, no poisons. If you have too many aphids, gently wipe them off with your fingers. Rub them out. If you have too many snails, then by all means, go pick them out of the plants they're hiding in and give them a proper burial in a mass grave (they make fine fertilizer). Lay some boards out among the plants and scrape the slugs off the undersides in the morning—but, please, do have break-fast first. You won't find all the snails and slugs, you won't smush all of the aphids, you won't be one hundred percent effective as an assas-sin, but you'll more closely imitate what nature does. And you'll cause less collateral damage as well.

It has often been said that American homeowners are the world's biggest polluters, that we urbanites use far more chemicals than our farmers do, mostly because there are so many more of us than farmers. But as we are descended from farmers, so too are we descended from farm traditions and it is this cultural legacy that gets us into trouble. Unlike you and I, a farmer relies on his plants to pro-vide him with an income. I can understand (although I am opposed to it) why a farmer opts for using pesticides and chemical fertilizers. If a farmer cannot keep ahead of wildlife, he <u>might</u> go broke. A farmer has a tractor salesman (who can basically charge whatever he wants for his machines) pulling at his left pocket and a purchasing agent (who creates the price that corn will be sold at) tugging out his right pocket. The farmer cannot control prices at either end. In his mind, he has ridiculously little room for error. A farmer can't afford pests or poor-looking crops. So, he uses poisons.

You at home, that's not your predicament. A couple of lost cucumbers are not the end of the world. You don't need to spray chemicals. It would be better, it seems to me, to learn how to take care of the cucumber plant so that it won't be set on by marauders. Smarter to study and adapt. Maybe, through observation, one of us backyard enthusiasts will discover a simple remedy for (fill in the pest) that won't involve killing. Maybe that discovery will be adopt-ed by progressive-thinking farmers. Maybe one of us will change the face of agriculture, thereby saving us all.

Other organic-minded gardeners have presented this philoso-phy of gardening so eloquently, in so many forums, that I am cha-grined to be borrowing their ideas, but, with a nod of appreciation, I strive to carry the torch. Like me, the pest is a messenger. Don't kill the messenger. Figure out what the messenger is saying. Heed the advice. Listen to the old timers who used to say, "Too many snails? Not enough ducks." Let the carnage stop with you.

"It would be sad if the
history of food were to
end with the word FAMINE."

History Of Food, Maguelonne Toussaint-Samat

A WORLD OF GRUB

My first professional garden was, naturally, behind the garage. Civilized people don't want to see "messy" tomatoes and "unruly" zucchini. Today hale and hardy weeds live in my incipient plot and not much else.

My second garden was set outside the kitchen --— perfect! But now, again, it has been transformed into something else. In this case the garden was removed entirely after a tree fell, revealing a panoramic vista to the sea. Ocean view or string beans? Hmm, what would you choose?

Yes, long ago there were small gardens in these locales. I learned fantastic things by tending those grounds, tricks and techniques that I still use today. I was allowed to experiment with someone else's sun and soil, given the chance to wrestle with critters I might never have faced had I stayed put in my own back forty feet. Now, hundreds of gardens later, I feel enormously changed.

The reason for writing these thoughts down is because those first gardens failed. Failed because I didn't share what I was experiencing. Not enough. Not enough to make a vegetable garden an indispensable necessity to them. They understood and appreciated good food, but they didn't have the dirt-under-the-nails, dirt-up-the-nose, dirt-in-your-underpants relationship with food that I did. So, I try to share what I know with you. And if I inspire you to break ground in a fully aware way, then . . . then . . . well, then I'll have done something.

For, you see, vegetables, fruits and herbs are, to me, the most unbelievable wonders on this planet. Forget the Seven Wonders of the World (if you haven't already). Dump Yosemite, Everest, the Sistine Chapel, Stonehenge, the Great Wall, and the Grand Canyon into a big pile over there, please. Dismiss anything you feast your eyes and ears on because for my money ($11.37) the only things that can keep company with crops are air, water, light, fire and gravity.

Heady company indeed.

I mean, just for a second, try getting your brain around a peach. A peach grows on a tree. We don't have to run like crazy to catch it. In fact, if you're chasing down peaches as a matter of habit, I'm gonna bet $11.37 you got dropped on your head once too often as a kid. A peach doesn't resist us, no, the tree advertises its fruit because if we don't eat the peaches and subsequently, if all the pits that fall upon the ground germinate and grow, they will crowd out the mother tree, crowd out each other and eventually that family of peaches might die out. The peach tree needs something to eat its fruit and move its seed to distant lands, and it really doesn't give a holler who does it. But think about it, rabbits don't really need us to eat them. Nor do cows. The redwoods don't need us to walk through them. The Nile doesn't need us to drink its waters. The Andes don't need us to smell their rarified air. Fiji sands don't need to slip through fingers. Sunsets don't need to be sighed at. But a peach! Eat a peach, thank you!! And corn? Don't get me started on corn. Modern corn would go extinct without mankind. We've bred corn for so many years now that the kernels on a cob would only produce a mass of grass, no stalks, probably no substantial silks, no babies. In a scant decade or so, good old corn goes into the archives. Corn absolutely needs us. Isn't it swell to feel needed?

What's more, the remarkable variety of foods available to eat astounds me. God and evolution could easily have provided us a mere five things to eat. The list might read:

1. amaranth
2. pine nuts
3. jackfruit
4. poke salet greens
5. yucca root

These five items would supply just adequate nutrition. We would get by. With five items on the menu, us people folk would most certainly grit our teeth and eat it. Heck, we would thank the gods for five foods; we could have been given one food, little ponds of spirulina to stuff our hungry gullets with. Fortunately, though, we have many choices.

The modern supermarket, on average, has eighty different types of fruits and vegetables for sale, and that is only scratching at the surface of what could be available. At last count there were over fifteen thousand species of plants that are in some way edible, of which about one hundred fifty (1%) have been cultivated for mass consumption. Whack me upside the head, I just heard, there are nearly eight thousand cultivars of apples. We didn't have to be given all of these options, but we were and that truly amazes me.

And you can cook them. Or eat them raw. Or dry them. Or press the oils out of them. Or squeeze the juices out of them. You can blend them or have them by themselves. You can stew, freeze, boil and nuke 'em. Some you need to eat all at once and some you can save for later. Some you can save for years and years (beans withdrawn from Egyptian tombs were planted, harvested and reportedly found to be quite yummy). There are gobs and gobs of edibles, each and every one as flexible as Gumby's pony pal Pokey. Amazing.

In the equatorial jungles there are no distinct seasons, foods grow year round. Acquiring a full belly can take no more effort than walking around a bit and eating what you see. Amazing.

In Alaska, the growing season is short but the days are long—twenty some hours long. In a few months time it is possible to grow cabbages large enough to cast an eclipse, carrots so big that they pull up parts of China when harvested, and onions so rotund that when they're sliced the entire population of Minnesota sheds tears (hence the ten thousand lakes). To the point, nature is going to provide. You've got a short growing season, no problem, nature'll just add more hours of sunlight, give you constant drizzle, a softening cloud cover, and that should just about do you. Food, food and more food. Doesn't it astound you? Remember, it doesn't have to be this way. But it is.

Vegetables, fruits, and herbs are here. And they feed us. They taste good. They can be nice to look at. Most importantly though, they change us. Physically they change us. Every biteful, every nutritious chomp, effects your body chemistry. There are few external things that alter your internal makeup. There are fewer external things that we have contact with so frequently that deliver such a wallop of enrichment.

Thus, I admit it, I stand in awe of the vegetable garden. To me, it is God's second most generous gift, the first being consciousness. But without the life-sustaining energy the garden provides me, my consciousness would wither and my flesh would soon return to the soil. Foods are inexorably linked to our existence. Everyone I know eats. Not everyone I know realizes how blessed we are. Someday though . . .

FOODS YOU CAN'T
BUY IN THE SUPERMARKET
so you grow them at home, don't ya know

1. pea tendrils
2. green seeds--fennel, cilantro, dill, mustard, onion
3. garlic scallions
4. guava blossoms
5. radish pods
6. pickled nasturtium seeds
7. dahlia root divisions
8. Malabar spinach fruits
9. fresh baby grape leaves
10. organic daylilies
11. rose hips
12. sourgrass, cheeseweed, chickweed
13. sesame leaves

S C A 2 Z

Read all about it. Try if you'd like. The books on vegetable gardening do not, cannot, cover the wild and wooly spectrum of knowledge it takes to grow foods in Southern California. Why's that?

- Everything grows here if you give it water.
- Just about everything short of tundra will survive in SoCal, some of it better than elsewhere, some of it not as well. That makes it difficult to figure out how to tend your papaya when it's sitting smack dab next to the bread-seed poppies, which, it just so happens, are sharing root space with the annual stevia.
- Unlike most areas of the known world, we are dry. Dry, dry, dry.
- We have alkaline soil.
- Our soil is an excellent material for making clay houses.
- Our winters are what most people think of as spring.
- Our frosts last for minutes at a time, sometimes seconds.
- We have the largest variety of immigrants in the world and consequently every type of food choice can be explored before planting—for instance, if you're not sure you want to plant bitter gourd, you can simply cruise down to Garden Grove and order it from one of the many Vietnamese takeout joints, sample it, consider whether or not you enjoy a vegetable that tastes like bile, drive home, and decide to grow it anyway because it's a downright beautiful plant. Try doing that in West Virginia (you could do it but, man, that's a long errand to go on).
- We have zero down time because our weather lets us grow year round, hence, we don't get to snuggle up by the fire with hot chocolate and pour over seed catalogs. No, dammit, we just have to work, work, work, work, work.

- ✑ We have the freshest produce in the country, so why grow it?
- ✑ We have thousands of good restaurants (at least eighty where I live alone) .Why cook?
- ✑ We have a huge, daily influx of visitors from southern countries who are willing to garden our gardens for chump change—why garden?

Because. Because we love to. Here's some stuff you might not find in the books.

A

ARTICHOKES. I can't tell you how many times people say to me, "We can grow artichokes here?" I don't know why this is so utterly amazing to folks, yet it is. Yes, we can. And they are a perfect choice for the front yard garden. They are graceful, grey (which contrasts well with other plants), they are spiky like phormium and/or acanthus, and they have a knockout flower. Artichokes prefer to be watered from above; they like to get their leaves wet. Artichokes attract aphids, but the aphids are brought there by ants (which farm them). Washing the plants free of aphids will help deter the ants; so will dropping crushed mint leaves into and around the artichoke plant. In fact, a spray of chilled mint tea is a generally good ant deterrent (no sugar added please). Artichokes will also be a great breeding ground for lady beetles. If you want ladies in your garden you'll need to allow some of the aphids to stay in your chokes—a girl's gotta eat don'tcha know. Once the artichoke flower opens, the number of honeybees visiting your garden will quadruple. The artichoke should be treated like a delphinium, in that the main stalk should be permitted to fall to the ground and dry up and a new "off-spring" shoot pop up from the old root before the plant is cleaned up. If the stalk is removed too early the longevity of the artichoke is reduced. Artichokes can be considered a short-lived perennial (seven to ten years).

AMARANTH. Amaranth is a staple green/grain throughout tropical regions of the world that is only now finding its way back into North American cuisine. From Africa to Asia the leaves are a daily green. Its tiny seeds are ground into flour and used in every manner traditional and exotic. In SoCal, there is no easier crop to grow. The plants are big and gaudy, with huge plumes of flower. They come in colors from gold to volcanic red. While the plant is growing, salads can be made from their numerous leaves. This is a nutritious plant and one that should be included in most gardens.

ALLSPICE. Allspice is a vain plant, "I'm <u>All</u> Spice, and don't you forget it." Allspice is native to North America. It grows here in sun or shade, as a small bush or as a tall hedge. It is fairly drought tolerant but likes water, too. It is a solid background plant. Crush a leaf and your nose is bombarded by Christmas memories. Make a tea, yum. This a perfect plant for SoCal and should be utilized accordingly.

B

BLUEBERRIES. Blueberries are a fruit that needs to chill. We don't chill here. But there are varieties that have been hybridized to need less chillin'. With names like "Star" and "Cape Fear" these blueberries do a good job of pretending to like it here. What I found to be most helpful after years of paltry crops and wimpy looking specimens is to put each new shrub into its own large pot or half whiskey barrel and plant it in straight peat moss. It is my anecdotal experience that blueberries cannot abide the alkaline soil we possess. Once a blueberry root hits alkaline it runs another direction or just stops growing right there in its tracks. I've had great success with peat moss.

BORAGE. Borage is a weed. Borage is pretty, the flowers taste like cucumbers but they never tell you until it's too late—Borage is a weeeeed!!

BEANS. Beans are invaluable but you must devote ample space to them in order to fill your belly. Climbing beans are great space savers and if you have any fence to spare, put them there. Bush beans really have the best variety of flavors though, so if you're a bean lover (like moi) then you'll be wantin' to mix it up with all sorts of beanage.

C

CALENDULA. Calendulas are loathed by many of my gardening pals, and I've never really figured out why. They note how much deadheading they take, how they're prone to getting leaf miners, how the colors are icky, but y'know, I think the benefits far outweigh those grumpy complaints. First, calendulas, like marigolds, exude nematode-fighting toxins into the soil but don't have the same acrid flavor in the flowers. And the flowers are why I love calendulas. The petals make any dreary salad special. They can be rolled into cream cheese or goat cheese and not effect the flavor. The flowers can be baked into muffins or bread and will hold their color so that bites of blueberry muffin can be speckled with bright yellow or orange. Lastly, they're easy. I just let them be, I rarely deadhead them, rarely pick clean infested leaves. I don't expect much from them and consequently, I love 'em.

CARDAMON. This tropical plant is best in dappled shade and does well in a pot. It's pretty, kind and courteous to strangers. Brush by this plant and the air fills with the scent of spices. This is a great plant to have by the path or the back door.

CILANTRO. Cilantro is sold at all the nurseries, at KMart, Wal-Mart and Bunch o'CrapMart every springtime. This is wrong. In SoCal, cilantro is a winter crop and should be sold in the fall. It seems to take just one day of eighty plus degrees for cilantro to start bolting. Here in L.A. we get a few eighty and over days. Green cilantro seeds are spectacular eating though. If your plant bolts, wait for the little green seeds and take the good with the bad.

CAPERS. Capers are drought tolerant. They are beautiful shrubs, covered with showy white flowers set against grey-green half-dollar-sized leaves. Given sufficient drainage the plants take care of themselves. And whereas ants are usually a problem for most of the SoCal garden, here, with capers, the ants actually help with pollination. Isn't it nice finally to have a plant that the ants can visit? I'm saddened by the genocidal ant attacks occurring with such regularity in our gardens. Hurray for the capers. Preparing the capers is not difficult, though it takes patience. A cup or so of berries are collected, rinsed and put into a container with sea salt. The berries need to be kept in the refrigerator, salted and stirred every day, for about two weeks. Then the capers are rinsed free of salt and pickled in your favorite vinegar overnight. The leaves can be pickled, too. It's a great plant.

CACTUS. Here we are in the desert, why not grow what grows best? Tuck some cacti into a desolate corner of your yard and learn to love it. Few edible plants require less attention and you'll look water-wise to your fanatic drought-tolerant buddies. Another great thing about cactus is that you rarely have to buy it—you can usually just snap some off from a friend or enemy's plant, carry it home and shove it into the ground. There are hundreds of ways of using the young flat pads (nopalitos) and of cooking up the brick-red fruits. If you can't find any good recipes walk down the block and ask the old Latina feeding the pigeons if she'll come over to your casa and give you some instructions.

CHOP SUEY. Chrysanthemum greens are a godsend in the edible landscape. To have a traditional looking flowering plant amongst the other oddballs lends legitimacy to your claim that edible landscaping can be beautiful. The plant grows fairly large (3' x 3') and produces bunches of flowers. The leaves are eaten in a variety of ways and are quite "spicy" when eaten raw. To me they have a slight pesticide smell due to my familiarity with pyrethrin (an "organic" pesticide derived from chrysanthemum leaves). No matter whether I like to eat the leaves or not, I still enjoy growing the plant for the flowers and for the comforting knowledge that if there were a famine, I'd have one more nasty tasting thing on hand to keep me alive.

CHAMOMILE. These seeds are hard to get going. Why? They like to freeze first. If you want a good crop of chamomile, buy the seeds and put them into the freezer for six weeks or so. Thawing out will help them to germinate. This is a good technique for many tiny cold-country seeds. Knowing where your plants grew originally will often help you to grow them better.

D

DAYLILIES. Daylilies are a common sight in SoCal gardens. Did you know that you can eat the flowers? Did you know that they come in all sorts of flavors? Some are sweet, some spicy, some taste like squash. They can be stir-fried or eaten raw. Dried daylily blossoms are added to soups. An entire flower can be put into a poached egg dish (stamen removed) and filled with melon balls or sorbet—which is so very Martha .

DANDELIONS. Eating dandelions is normal. Get used to it. You'll thank me for it. Dandelions are fairly easy to grow and the pisenlit (red-stemmed and actually a chicory) variety is quite attractive. The difficult aspect to growing dandelions is the removal of the flowers so as to reduce the number of volunteers you have growing in you garden the next year. What to do? Eat the flowers. Yep, make a simple egg and flour batter, roll the yellow, freshly picked flowers in the batter and fry them up. Easy, good and different. If you don't want to pick or eat the flowers you can take comfort in the fact that the dandelion is a marvelous attractor of beneficial insects.

E

EARLY. Water your precious babies early in the day. In the Southwest, plant seeds earlier than the package says you can. All hybrids with the name "Early" in their title, such as Early Girl tomato, Early cantaloupe, Early sweet corn, can be transplanted in September and harvested between Thanksgiving and Christmas. My cool season crops usually include some Earlies.

ENDIVE. Endive is a no-brainer. It is a beautiful plant that can grace the edges of the path or the heart of the bed beneath the birdbath. If you must blanch it to remove the bitterness, it will be easier to plant endive away from your other crops so that you'll have space to maneuver around the plants. I like endive as a plant first and as an edible second.

F

FIGS. Easy as pie. Black Mission is the most common but there are many. They can grow to be quite large trees but what I like about fig trees is their adaptability. They can be kept quite small and still produce enough figs for the average bear. They can be espaliered. They will grow in partial shade or blasting sun. Because we are so arid here in the summer, figs can be sliced up, put on a cookie sheet and left to dry out in the sun and then eaten with roasted almonds. Real good.

FENNEL. Fennel grows wild here by the beaches. Bronze fennel is a terrific landscape plant as its airy fronds play nicely against the more dense foliage of neighbors. The bulbs are known to be great with fish, but I like fennel/potato soup myself. I also cherish the times when the fat seeds appear on the bush and I get to direct kids to the "candy plant." Once, when I was at the Huntington Botanical Gardens with some friends, I got to share the candy plant with a little guy about five years old. "Here, Chris, taste this," I said. "It tastes like candy." He took the seeds from my palm, looked around furtively and answered, "Okay, but don't tell my Dad."

FREEZES. In the event that a frost is coming our way, if the nightly news warns that we might have to take our sweaters out of storage, know that our freezes don't last but overnight. If you hose down any frost tender plant the evening of a predicted freeze, the water on the leaves will act as insulation against the cold. I know this sounds counter-intuitive but it is quite effective in application. Tiny sprouts can be gently covered with a cloth and they should have a fairly good survival rate as well. If you do lose new plantings, don't cry, you'll rarely have to go through this experience again in SoCal. I mean, admit it, we have bitchen weather here. Got some chill? No worries, hombre. Says young Jesse, "The days'll be like tight again fully in like hours. Sweet!"

FIDDLEHEADS. Fiddle-dee-dee indeed. If you've got a good spot for ferns then you've got a good spot for fiddleheads. As the new ferns emerge coiled and delicate you can snip a few away from the plant and toss them into your steamer or stir-fry (you'll probably not want to eat them raw). Most species of fern have edible fiddleheads, but ostrich fern is the most commonly eaten one (at least here in the States). As I always say, when you add something that is visually dynamic to your meal you're also adding flair to your life.

G

GINGKO. Gingko trees are primordial and provide the herbal supplement Gingko Bilbo Baggins. Small gingko leaves can be added to salads. Many people eat the seeds although squirrels seem to get the most. This is a great tree for us here because it turns lemon yellow in the fall, adapts well to our soils and does not overwhelm the landscape. I love the grounds covered with fallen gingko leaves. The fact that it has edible parts is just gravy.

GRAPES. Another indispensable landscape plant. I have friends who have a vineyard in their backyard. They make award-winning wines (eight hundred fifty bottles worth this year) and they make some dynamite grappa. Their backyard is large enough to have had a pool and tennis court and a small garden. Instead they have a vine-yard, a small orchard, a nice garden. The thing about grapes though is that they can be trained any old way—up a trellis, along the fence, as a tree, as a mess behind the garage. Grapes are low water, low maintenance. I like to pick the young leaves and eat them on the spot. The trick to pruning so that clusters of fruit will form near the woody vines is quite simple. Just as you would with a climbing rose, cut back each branching cane about a half an inch above the second bud (so the bud doesn't accidentally dry out), and the plant will produce bunches closer to the main stem. The saying from the "old country" goes, "two on the vine, eight in the bottle."

GARLIC. The garlic capital of the U.S. is Gilroy, around seventy miles south of San Francisco and smack-dab in Steinbeck country. The garlic we find in our supermarkets is Gilroy garlic. There are many, many, many kinds of garlic to grow and an entire book can be (and has been) devoted to them, but I always choose to plant some basic supermarket garlic. Why? The greens and the flowers. Both the green scallions and the seeds have a strong garlic flavor and you can't buy either at the market. While you're waiting for the bulb to form you can cut the scallions. Once the bulb has flowered you can take the seeds and sprinkle them in your food.

H

HORSERADISH. Watch out. You may think that you like horseradish and want to grow some, but it will not be the same wussy horseradish they sell in the store. Home-grown paint remover is what it should be called. Homemade horseradish spread, undiluted, is a great gift for your enemies. Conspiracy theorists believe that the monks assigned to watch over Napoleon on his prison isle slowly killed him by adding small doses of arsenic to his food on a daily basis. I say, bosh, rubbish. The Little Emperor was killed by horseradish.

HEIRLOOMS. I get asked often enough that I feel I should make the case for heirlooms. Heirlooms, as you know, are plants that have been saved by families for many generations, passed down, grown for their unique qualities by a long line of enthusiasts. As most of our world has been industrialized and commercialized, so has the business of seeds. Most of the seeds in the world are "owned" by corporations. In order to grow most plants a grower has to buy his seeds from these companies. One of the companies is named Seminis, and their main offices are located here in SoCal. The owner of Seminis is one of the wealthiest men in the world. Most of the seeds sold by corporations are hybrid plants, meaning that their offspring, the seeds produced by these plants, won't always grow true. For instance, a Better Boy tomato will produce seeds, plenty of them, but if you were to save and plant those seeds next season you'd not likely get a Better Boy, you'd probably just get a Boy or maybe, y'know, a Lesser Boy. With heirlooms you'll always grow true. A Black Sea Man tomato (don't say that too fast) will always produce more Black Sea Man. Corporations don't "own" heirlooms. Corporations want control over their product. Corporations want you to come back and buy their product year after year. I recommend that you cast your vote for the little guy. Buy and plant heirlooms.

I

INLAND/OUTLAND. We drive so much in L.A. that we forget how far we're traveling. Growing up, my mom was forbidden to make the long drive to Fargo—it was forty miles. Hell, most of us do forty in our sleep (which explains our goofy traffic). Anyway, the point is, we have ten different microclimates to contend with. Knowing your zone will help you choose plants that are going to do better. For instance, if you live in Malibu and are deciding upon tomatoes at the annual Tomato Mania® and the label for Arkansas Traveler says the fruit loves heat, pass on by and keep shopping until you land upon a German tomato like Brandywine and go for that. Brandywine tomatoes fruit and taste best when daytime temps are around eighty degrees. Brandywines struggle in Chatsworth. Beans love Riverside. Peppers love Culver City. Cukes like Compton. Lettuce likes Laguna. You get the picture.

ISHI. Back in the olden days, about 1911 or so (when the world was still organic), a tired and gaunt Indian stumbled out of the hills surrounding Mount Lassen, California, and gave himself up to the White Man. Ishi was the last surviving member of his tribe, the Yana. The others had been slaughtered and traded by land developers of the past (we call them pioneers). Ishi was befriended by scientists and given a home in a museum and was a big attraction with the hoi-poloi of San Francisco until he died of tuberculosis.

"And?" you're wondering. "So?"

My parents, and I don't know why, had a copy of Ishi's biography on the family bookshelf. As a kid I found the photos of old Ishi in his loincloth spearing fish to be quite comical. But Ishi also made me realize that for thousands, if not millions of years, people had lived on wild foods. Stepping out of your hut and chewing on a nearby plant was a normal pastime for most of our forebears. Ishi made me look at my environment with new eyes. Ishi gave me permission to experiment with edibles. And I'm suggesting that you act a little more like Ishi, too. When your husband asks you why you're topless and eating weeds in the yard just answer defiantly, "Ishi."

IVY. Algerian ivy was so popular as a ground cover in the 1960s that it became ubiquitous. I would argue that Algerian ivy could be found more often than palm trees or even oranges in a SoCal garden. And what a pity. What a waste of space. Say, you know, I've got an idea. Get rid of it!! True, it's drought tolerant, but so is thyme and oregano and rosemary. True, it's evergreen, but bougainvillea is prettier. True, it's great for breeding rats, but . . . exactly!! It's great for breeding rats! Get rid of it! Wondering where to put in all of these wonderful plants I'm recommending? Put them where the ivy WAS!! Get rid of it!!! (Please obtain your doctor's permission before attempting to remove a swath of insidious ivy.) Did I mention to GET RID OF IT?!!!!

J

JICAMA. This versatile tuber comes from Central America and as a plant is sometimes sold as "yam bean." I've found that you can usually get a laugh if you refer to someone who deserves it as "stupid as a yam bean." In the countries where jicama grows naturally it is harvested rather small—about the size of a baseball. The commercial jicama that we get at the supermarket, I am told by mi amigo Candelario, are not only Godzilla-like absurdities but they are bland, cardboard-tasting embarrassments. Kind of reminds you of the complaints folks make about tomatoes, doesn't it?

Growing jicama is fun. Seeds are available from nurseries and on-line. Jicama is a climbing vine and should be seeded in the late winter—somewhere around February or March. I get better results with a slightly more acid soil mix. Harvest a root when the vines start flowering and harvest one after it has set seed pods and determine which is more flavorful. Remember that your jicama will be small compared to the market variety, but, hey, who else do you know who is growing jicama?

JUJUBE. When I talk about jujubes, people often think I'm referring to the chewy candy that can be found at movie theatres—the candy that when thrown at the screen sticks indefinitely. I clearly remember a jujube clinging beneath Meryl Streep's nostrils for most of *Sophie's Choice*. But that ain't the jujube I'm talking about. I'm talking about a tree. Talkin' 'bout a tree that produces fruits that taste like dates but are crunchy like apples. Jujubes love it dry and hot. They need water, but they like to bake otherwise. Jujubes grow straight and tall and consequently are a nice landscape plant. Jujubes are perfect for SoCal.

K

KELP. Lots of old-time Rodale-heads swear by kelp. I just swear. Kelp, if it's clean, is an excellent addition to your compost because it contains so many trace minerals. One guy I know fills a fifty-gallon drum with water and kelp, lets it "cure" for a year and uses that exclusively on his garden—and it works just dandy. It does smell like an old wet pig though, I won't lie to you. Kelp is a top-notch fertilizer when mixed with a manure tea and it's cheap if the lifeguards don't catch you harvesting it. You can buy liquid kelp, too. The commercial stuff comes from arguably cleaner waters than our own but it can be pricey. A fifty-gallon drum of the stuff would cost you, like, a billion dollars or something. One idea might be to buy a house on the beach in Malibu and have your own source of seaweed. Then, if you had some extra you could give some at Christmastime to Barbra Streisand, or Johnny Carson, or Pamela Anderson—you know, your neighbors. Just an idea.

KIWI. This vine, once established, grows like the dickens. When the plant is young, however, it grows more like Emily Dickinson—spare and fussy. This is a great plant for covering fences between properties or for covering pergolas. One male plant can pollinate five or six females, but you'll need to remember to buy both a boy <u>and</u> a girl when you start out. These plants do need water and good soil. Do not skimp on anything when you transplant them into their spots. They may burn initially but just keep them regularly watered and within a year or two you'll be reaping the rewards.

KUMQUATS. Maybe my favorite citrus. These guys are ornamental. They have fruit most of the year. They are great when juiced and made into an "ade." They stir-fry. They freeze into perfect BBs for your slingshot. When I was a kid, my sister, our friends, and me would see who could get the most kumquats in our mouth and then eat them all. I think Annie Carruthers got twenty-seven in her mouth once. You won't regret planting a kumquat.

KOHLRABI is a nice addition to the winter vegetable garden. It's all edible, leaves and bulb, and it's best when served raw. Mixing kohlrabi and jicama "fries" on a raw vegetable platter, dipped or smeared with something cheesy-like is a great way to go. Kohlrabi gets less attention from cabbage looper butterflies and thus has nary a pest problem here in SoCal. The purplish hues of purple kohlrabi contrast nicely in the landscape and the bulbous stem atop the soil has a fun, Dr. Seuss quality I like.

L

LEMON GRASS. This herb is used in lots of Asian cooking. It's a tempting plant to add to your shopping basket at the nursery because when it's small and dainty it has a delicate lemon scent. Don't be fooled though. Lemon grass grows into a big, big clump. It's attractive if placed properly, but that's the key. Put it outside of the herb garden, on the borders, as a background plant. Don't sock it smack dab in the front and hope it stays small. It won't.

LEMON BALM. A pretty lime-green ground cover that has a nice lemony aroma. Some folks take cuttings of this with them on camping trips and rub it all over themselves to deter mosquitoes. This herb has traditionally been steeped as a breakfast tea and informally linked to extended longevity. For some reason or another, people who drink lemon balm tea often live longer than people who smoke cigarettes and exchange hypodermic needles with strangers do. Go figure.

LEMON VERBENA. Another nice "lemony-fresh" addition to your garden. I almost always plant this in new gardens. As the plant ages it grows quite tall and can be trained into a small tree. It is used with all types of cooking, and the flowers are a "good" insect attractor. Sticking the leaves up your nose makes kids laugh.

LEEKS are my favorite plants in the landscape. I treasure their giant flowers above all others. The sight of a dozen or so "towers of leek" truly makes me giddy. You can buy leeks at the supermarket, dirty and chopped, take them home, stick them in the soil and have a veritable leek forest by fall. Oh, by the way, you can eat them, too.

M

MALABAR SPINACH is a fantastic summer annual that self-seeds so well you'd swear it was a perennial. The vine can easily grow twenty feet between April and September. The skin of the plants I grow (*Basella rubra*) are an electric fuschia color. The reddish/purplish hue of the vine is what I enjoy most. The leaves taste somewhat like Swiss chard with a hint of lemon and like okra are slimy (mucilaginous). I rarely eat the leaves and stems because I prefer the end of the season fruits. They are almost black and about the size of a caper. They have a sweet beet flavor and when they're sprinkled over salads they never fail to please.

MURPHY'S OIL. Bullets should cost more. Chris Rock has it right—each bullet should cost $5,000. "I'm gonna kill your ass. I'm gonna get me another job, maybe two jobs and get the money for a bullet. You better pray I can't get no bullet on lay-away." One common bullet of the organic crowd is paraffin or vegetable oil. Another bullet is soap—both botanical and household. If you want to control a wide variety of insects in both adult and egg stage, Murphy's Oil is the ticket. And it's cheaper than any similar product you'll buy at the nursery. When push comes to shove, when I've failed at creating a natural balance, I will start over with Murphy's Oil.

MACHE. Mache is a domesticated weed used in salads extensively throughout Europe. Mache (pronounced "mosh") sprouts up just about everywhere the season after it is first introduced to your garden. A big bowl of freshly picked mache with a splash of olive oil, a lemon squeezed over it and some good hard cheese on the side is against the law in several of the Plains states, er, I mean, it ought to be.

MINER'S LETTUCE. This green is pretty yummy but not so easy, in my experience, to germinate. You'll find that this plant, like many natives, only wishes to grow in spots it has personally selected. If you get miner's lettuce popping up in your garden be sure to use it in your salads and whatnot. Unless you have so much miner's lettuce that you could choke a goat I would never try to eradicate it—I would give thanks to Jack in the Green, I would. This is a good plant to go looking for when you're pretending to be Ishi.

N

NASTIES. Nasturtiums are one of the most common edible flowers. While the flower can be eaten, I like to point out that so, too, can the leaves and the seeds. The seeds can also be pickled and served as a spicy hot side dish. Nasturtiums are not in the watercress family but taste so similar that many people think they are related (kind of like how people assume Brad Pitt and me are brothers). Another benefit to growing nasturtiums is that they attract gobs of aphids and can be used to keep the suckers from invading other plants. Look for the offbeat nasturtium varieties sold by seed and you'll be happier. Nasturtiums will do well in shade.

NICE. Our climate is nicer than Nice's. Nice's is nice but ours is nicer.

O

OKRA may well be one of the prettiest crop plants you can grow. It has a beautiful flower on a thin, spindly stalk that appears at the hottest time of the year. So, in August when every other plant is gasping for life, okra is lighting it up. If you plant the red-stemmed okra you are also adding one more vibrant color to your summer landscape. Oh, yeah, some people like to eat the pods, too.

ORACH. In the winter our gardens can get a wee predictable. Here we plant the crucifers, the greens, the roots, and the tubers in the fall. Orach is a plant that gives your winter a touch of the exotic. Orach can get quite big in the right spot, and comes in a lovely mix of pinks and reds and pale greens. It's good in salads, soups and stir-fries. One particularly good salad mixes it with sorrel, mache and roasted hazelnuts.

OLEANDER. My mom was so deathly afraid that one of her kids would get poisoned by our oleander trees that she had a Haz Mat scrub tent installed on our patio so that we could sanitize ourselves immediately after touching a leaf. We were told that a prized racehorse had once eaten from our trees and summarily died in our driveway. I've learned as an adult to be less frightened of these poisonous trees. But oleanders are everywhere, as are azaleas, wisteria, foxglove and other toxic plants and I am asked constantly if the poisons in these plants are absorbed by nearby edibles. My answer is probably not. The important thing is to be sensible but not paranoiac. If you have a choice don't plant right next to these plants. If you pick up an oleander twig, don't clean your teeth with it. Don't bathe in azalea water; don't staunch a puncture wound with wisteria leaves.

P

PARSLEY is the perfect addition to every garden, formal or wild. Electric-green Italian parsley plays so well with others. Traditional, tight-curled parsley looks great with the pansies and ornamental kale. Parsley's uses number in the thousands but I really love having it on hand in the summer when I do a lot of juicing. Watermelon, juiced with apple, garlic and parsley is one of my personal favorites.

POTATOES. I buy my seed potatoes at the health food store. I put them in a mesh bag in a cupboard and wait for them to sprout. Once they've sprouted I could cut them up, but I don't bother, I just take them out to the garden and plant them whole. I plant them in the fall. As the vines grow you can pile mulch up around them, leaving only the faintest trace of vegetation visible, and the potatoes will set tubers along the vine under the mulch. Sometimes I practice this technique, sometimes not. When I finally harvest potatoes (after the foliage has yellowed and begun to die), I dig them all up, separate the boys from the men and put all the boys straight back into the soil. I then amend with compost and the cycle begins again. Only in the hottest part of the summer does my little potato engine slow down.

POMEGRANATES. If you're looking for an easy and showy ornamental edible for SoCal, look to the pomegranate. Pomegranates can be trained as a small shrub, a big shrub or a tree. They can be espaliered. Pomegranate juice is trendy right now but my feeling is trendy or not there will never be anything better for ruining a nice angora sweater than a juicy pomegranate. I love pomegranates.

PALM HEARTS. When the wind blows here I get palm seeds all over everything. Bordering our property are ten palm trees, seventy-five feet tall, that were, no doubt, installed to entice wayward Oklahomans to my neighborhood some ninety years ago. One year, after a particularly brutal windstorm, I collected five five-gallon buckets of palm seeds from my driveway. Twenty-five gallons of seeds. You can imagine then how many volunteer palms I have had to deal with. Until recently I cursed these invaders, now I eat them. When they get about a foot high I dig them up and slice them up. Another way of turning something bad into something good.

Q

QUINCE. People love to grow quince trees and I must admit to loving their floral explosion. My problem with quince in SoCal is global warming. I'm sure somebody somewhere in SoCal is growing really tasty quince, just not me. I think it's just too bloody hot here. If you must have a quince in order to feel complete, by all means, go ahead and stick it in your dirt. Just don't expect the fruit you remember from the "old country."

QUESTIONS. Learn to ask the right questions. It's not, "What's wrong with my plant that I keep getting aphids?" It's, "What's wrong with my soil that my plant keeps getting aphids?" It's not, "How can I fix this?" It's, "How does nature fix this?" Don't ask, "How can I get more out of my garden?" Ask, "How can I give more to my garden?"

R

RADISHES are good eatin'. Radish pods are better. Each radish puts out twenty to fifty small green pods that taste like mild radishes. The pods are harvestable for only a few days so they are truly a treat. Sprinkled in salads, the little pods are one of those happy surprises that delight dinner guests, similar in fun to having a wild squirrel chased across the dining room table by a manic Jack Russell terrier.

RHUBARB. There seems to be a universal hankering for a rhubarb and strawberry pie in late summer. People ask me every year to plant rhubarb, and I tell them that it doesn't get cold enough here to make the stalks super-tasty. We plant it anyway. It's got a terrific flower and is a superb background plant in and amongst the landscape. I keep it out of the traditional veggie garden—it takes up too much space. You'll often read that rhubarb is poisonous, and it is, but you would need to eat nine pounds of the leaves before it would kill you. As my brother likes to point out, nine pounds of Big Macs would probably kill you, too.

S

SWEET PEAS. Two things about sweet peas. I plant them with sugar snap peas to deter and confuse pea-eating pests. Sometimes it works. I plant climbing beans on the same trellises and tepees where peas have just finished (peas in the winter, beans in the summer). Instead of throwing the sweet pea vines into the compost, I chop them up on the spot, seedpods and all, and use them to mulch my beans. The pea seeds tend to germinate soon thereafter and are shaded by the beans throughout the early summer. This strategy has helped me to have sweet peas in full swing by September and in bloom by Christmas.

SOUPY SALES. Uh, no comment.

SEASONS. We do kind of have seasons here. Hot and hotter and one really cold day. Think of seasonal planting this way—in the cooler months we eat primarily leaves and roots (except for broccoli, cauliflower—which both happen to have yummy leaves—and peas) and in the warmer months we eat flowers, fruits and seeds (e.g. artichoke, tomatoes and beans). If you know what part of the plant you want to eat, you can generally deduce what part of the year it should be planted in SoCal. If you live elsewhere, you plant in the spring after that stuff called snow has melted.

SCORZONERA is a dark-brown, fleshy root that grows much like parsnips but is known for its slight oyster-like flavor. I had tremendous difficulty getting scorzonera to germinate until a seed package accidentally blew onto a gravel path and scattered its contents amongst the pebbles. Holy smokes, did I get a beautiful crop in that gravel. The flower is, at the risk of sounding gay, simply gorgeous. I mean, just fabulous! Can I tell you, it gives the whole bed that extra "jhuujzh" it is so desperately crying out for? Should you plant it? Girl, please.

SHISO. Also known as *perilla*, shiso is a plant that I have used ornamentally for years. The leaves are distinctly flavored and are great for sushi. Mostly I use this plant for the size and contrast it creates in a garden and as another "good" bug attractor.

T

TEA. You can grow your own tea here in SoCal. Tea is made from camellia leaves—*Camellia sinensis*, to be exact. It is nice to pick delicate new growth once a year and have yourself a ceremonial teapot of rare white-tip green tea. Tea camellias grow even better where it's more humid. Hence, we have no tea plantations here, but the plants do grow well enough to treat you to a cup or two every so often.

TARRAGON. One chef that I work with demands lots of tarragon in the garden. Before working with him I hadn't grown tarragon because, personally, I don't like the taste. Funny though, like so many plants, once I started to grow it and tasted it fresh, I grew to like it. I don't love it. I like it. It is definitely an easy and forgiving plant to grow. It's good in pots, too. If you like using tarragon in recipes, it is a must in the home patch.

THYME is one of those plants, like parsley, that should be tucked in all over the garden. Even if you only pick thyme once in a tortilla moon you should still incorporate it into your garden plan. And there are so many varieties: lemon, elfin, wooly, English, lime, variegated. Please, don't plant thyme around your sundial. Enough with the garden puns already.

TOMATOES. You've heard plenty about tomatoes, no doubt. Have you heard that it'd be a good idea to save the old plants for mulching next year's plants? Yep, tomatoes are narcissistic—loving to be mulched with their own kind. Another tomato secret is to take live vine cuttings, blend them, strain them and then spray them onto your roses. This act both protects and heals your roses of blackspot.

U

UPLAND CRESS. For those of you who like watercress, here's the answer. Upland cress doesn't have the "running water" requirement that watercress does but has nearly the same flavor when harvested. It still likes a good amount of moisture though, at least in my experience. It works nicely as living mulch under bigger plants like broccoli and turnips.

UMBRELLAS. It's not unusual to have a hot spell in the fall or winter here in SoCal and often they happen right when the seedlings are coming up (instead of frost we get heat). One technique I will use to protect babies is to water them well, open up an old, discarded umbrella with its u-shaped handle removed and spike it into the ground above the seedlings. Watering first is important because most of the cast-off umbrellas are black and absorb heat. I don't push the umbrella too close to the ground (I still want airflow), as I am only interested in creating a bit of shade. A bunch of umbrellas in the garden is a whimsical touch to be sure. You can explain that they are your homage to the artist Christof.

V

VARIEGATED. If you want to design a pretty vegetable garden then use as many variegated plants as possible. Face it, vegetable gardens tend to be green and greener. The more shapes and colors and textures you can add to the garden the better. Variegation is a design tool that is always at your disposal. Surprisingly, there are few plants that don't have a variegated variety available in the nurseries and/or seed catalogs.

VINES. Growing two or three vines together on the same structure will reduce the productivity of each plant but create a visually mesmerizing centerpiece to your garden. For instance, a combination of runner beans, Malabar spinach and lemon cucumbers is fully cool. The number of oddball mixtures is endless. Don't be afraid, little girl. Try it. You'll see.

VIPERS. Snakes are good. So are spiders. Don't kill them, just watch out you don't sit on them. Lizards are good, too. So are bees. Please learn to appreciate how each species has its own useful place in the garden. You do, however, have my permission to hate pigeons.

W

WATER. Our biggest issue in SoCal gardening is water. As long as people live here, water and who gets it will be a problem. I try to stay out of the ruckus. I suggest that you plant the majority of your landscape with natives and other drought-tolerant plants and then use your water quota on your edibles. It also might behoove you to convince your neighbors to go entirely native so that you can also use their water quota on your entirely edible landscape. Just make sure to share your harvest.

I also believe that every small garden needs a water feature both for practical and aesthetic purposes. Gardens "fertilized" with pond water thrive. Beneficial insects will come to your garden and stay if you have a pond for them to drink from. Goldfish will do well in a SoCal garden pond and will take care of the mosquitoes.

A pond makes a garden feel complete.

X

XTREME GARDENING. People tend to imitate rather than create. I hope, in reading this book, you've been inspired to create something new in your garden. An Xtreme garden might be one devoted not to plants that attract birds but one that attracts gnarly bugs—all kinds—a "bug garden." An Xtreme garden might be one filled with thousands of sticks of varying sizes shoved into the ground and painted in primary colors. An Xtreme garden might be a gravel bed with one stalk of strawberry corn growing from its center. An Xtreme garden might be mulched with promotional CDs. Anything daring would be X. Why an Xtreme garden? Because it's your space, your time, your life. For God's sake, have fun.

Y

YUCCA. If you have yucca in your proximity you then have a wonderful source for building garden structures. When the flower stalks have dried and seeded, you can easily cut ten-foot-long poles from the yucca and make bean tepees with them. I enjoy how rustic yucca poles look. What's more, the poles are feather light. Having only a pithy, dry core, they can be "pinned" together with long nails simply by pushing the nails through by hand. The poles last only a season, but they then can go into the compost and finish off a nice life cycle. Yucca root is a delicacy with a long southwestern history. It's delicious in soups, but I must admit never to have harvested it myself. I've only bought it at the market.

YELLOW DOCK is a common garden weed that you should incorporate into your salads. It has a strong, bitter sorrel flavor, but I think it is the mind of an enlightened gardener that elevates a lowly weed to a cherished cooking green. (All Hail Emerson!) Eating yellow dock also, shhh, saves you the trouble of weeding it away.

Z

ZUCCHINI. There are several ways to avoid the classic zucchini boat dilemma. First, accustom yourself to eating the flowers. Squash flowers have many uses but I like the simple zucchini quesadilla. A flower with some cheese (soy cheese, please) stuffed in, a dash of Dash tossed on, popped into the oven for a couple of minutes and voila, *c'est finis et trés magnifique*! A variety of zuke that is worth trying is called "Eight Ball." Eight Ball grows melon-sized zucchini that are easy to stuff. You also won't be stumbling upon as many giants with Eight Ball. Another good choice is golden zucchini. Finally, if you do find yourself late in the season with dozens of gargantuan zucchinis please don't offer them to your neighbors. You'll just be proving to them the supposed folly of vegetable gardening. Instead, get out a compass and construct a replica of Stonehenge and dance around it during the Autumnal Equinox (much like Ishi would have). That'll show those neighbors what fun a vegetable garden can be, won't it?

ZULUS. I once saw a documentary that profiled the African Zulus and their centuries-old relationship to the land. Sadly, many of the tribe was starving to death, and this was attributed to the Zulus' reluctance to eat foods unfamiliar to their culture. The film though, in an arrogant, western way, suggested that the Zulus were stupid, perhaps even inferior, for not adopting a new, modern diet. I wasn't sold. I know that we are not much better. We Americans still consume massive amounts of junk food simply out of habit. And our "good" food, in the main, is not as wholesome and nutritious as we pretend it is. Maybe the Zulus felt it was better to starve than to swallow the garbage we call food. I don't know. What I do know is that by growing some of your own food you will connect to a bigger picture of life.

ZSA-ZSA. Dahlink, you simply must join me and the boys, Hassock and Betyar in a flute of Gewürztraminer, won't you? Then, ahfter we have pahrtied you can noodle off and plant your mahvelous garden. Come, Dahlink.

"Never eat anything
bigger than your head."

SAK

THE TWENTY-MINUTE RULE

Midway through most of my talks I see a raised hand that is connected to the question, "Mr. Master Vegetablarian sir, I'm wondering how am I going to do all this stuff you're suggesting? I mean, where in the world am I gonna find time to put paper bags over all my pears so they'll ripen unscathed? And do you really think I'm gonna prune the grapes and the crepe myrtles now that I've got this titanium hip and, AND, how do you expect me to turn the compost pile and play my round of golf all in the limited time I've got? Quite honestly, Mister BaldyHead, you're starting to bug me what with all these chores you've got me doing."

There's always a thorn in the crowd. Luckily I've learned how to respond to the prickly ones. My first answer is simple. Don't worry about it. Worry and frustration are death to a great garden. Worry leads to resentment. Frustration leads to neglect. Neither resentment nor neglect is helpful to you or your garden. Gardening is fun. Forgiving. Liberating. Peaceful. Don't worry about your time—just do what you can, when you can.

Then comes my second answer. I pause dramatically, look about thoughtfully, all the while smiling like a tomcat with a mouthful of Tweety. It drives people nutty. I take a sip of lukewarm tea and then I give them answer B.

Twenty minutes a day. Twenty a day, no more, no less. Fifteen minutes of labor, five for cleaning up. Fifteen minutes of honest labor per day in your garden (Sundays off for important things like watching NASCAR) amounts to one hour thirty minutes per week. Multiply that by fifty weeks per year (minus the two weeks you're on holiday in Tuscany eating figs stuffed with roasted almonds, thyme and feta from goats you know personally, sipping bathtub grappa with the nicotine-stained mayor, and listening to seductive melodies plucked out on a boxy guitar by Enzo) and you will have spent seventy-five hours working in your garden. How much do you think you could accomplish with seventy-five hours at your disposal?

Many people can't get into the habit of twenty minutes per day. For them I refer back to answer A. Many other people have never considered the idea of working in their garden this way. But I remind them of their years of school when their entire day was blocked off into bite-sized portions, every task tackled step-by-step. Only as adults, when we entered into the busyness of business, did we find ourselves swamped with projects that ran for hours and days and weeks at a time. Only when we grew up did we have no time for fun. I say get a huge electric bell, mount it outside your back door and set it to ring at the end of "Gardening." I say hire yourself a mean old sea-hag to hand you a demerit every time you linger in the garden. Maybe she'll give you detention, too. She could call your parents and get you totally busted. Maybe if you worked too long, or too little, it would go on your permanent record.

I learned the Twenty-Minute Rule from an old guy with a magical garden in Montrose. To be quite frank, his garden was on the ordinary side—impatiens, camellias, sword ferns, roses, an orange tree, a lemon tree, grass. Nothing bold or exotic danced through his space. But his garden sang. It rocked. It was the tightest garden I've ever seen. The garden wasn't sterile, nor did it have a museum no-touch quality. His garden was warm and comfortable. Spider webs were everywhere. Butterflies and hummingbirds swept in and out. Beneath the shrubs was dense, rich leaf mulch. All the plants were expertly deadheaded, the tree branches hung just so, the grass was the mother of all greens.

On my first visit to his garden (I was there to prune out the upper branches of his orange and lemon trees since he was feeling less secure atop ladders) I noticed a large pile of camellia blossoms sitting on the patio bricks. I asked the old dude if he wanted me to put the blossoms into the trash for him. (Camellia blossoms are one of the few things I don't compost. They are notorious disease carriers.) He responded, "Nope, that's for tomorrow. Ran outta time this morning."

"I'll do it if you want," I hollered down from atop the Meyer.

He shook his head knowingly, "Nope. That's for me. They'll be part of tomorrow's twenty." He went back into his house, leaving me to ponder "tomorrow's twenty." I monkeyed about those trees for some time before I understood. Twenty minutes a day had produced a spectacular garden.

I've tried the Twenty-Minute Rule at my house. You'd think it would be easy, me being a professional muckety-muck gardener and all. But I admit it's a tough row to hoe. I'm always gardening for others. My garden is seldom my first priority. But the weeks when I have attempted to follow this technique have overwhelmingly convinced me of the efficacy of the Twenty-Minute Rule. Someday, I'll make it my habit. 'Til then, I'll go with answer A.

"If you *believe* your own claim to miracle doing and are sincere in your work, you are bound to succeed."

Harry Houdini

AIN'T KNOW HOW 'BOUT IT

You might think the focus of this project would be on supplying you with sage guidance, informing you on how to grow the best edible garden in the world-famous "Mr. Tony, Master Vegetablarian" style. Yes, you might think that. When I told people I was writing a book, invariably they asked, "Are you gonna talk about rotating peas? Tell us how much fish to spray? And why is it radishes get so dang hot and woody?" And I said, "Yep, probably." But I haven't done that. There are so many other books that do all that. I'd rather get you to think about the garden. I'd prefer to inspire you to veg. I want to get you out of the house and into the shed and out of the shed and into the dirt—in that order.

Lots of people will never garden because "they don't know how." They would rather hire me and folks like me who have been trained to "know how" to do it for them. Others will believe, "I know what I like when I see it, but I don't know how to make it that way." "I'm not creative." "I'm not good with colors like you." "Everything I plant dies." "I have a black thumb." "I need really good photos to work from or else I'm lost." And to them I say it's all true. It's true because you say so, dammit. Yes, by gum by golly, you are terribly aware of your limitations and it is incredibly important to be terribly aware of your limitations so that you can go out there, roll up your sleeves and limit yourself with vigor. Otherwise, heaven forbid, you'd be limitless and that would be mighty inconvenient now wouldn't it?

Uh, sorry. There I go spoutin' off again.

Often, when someone is touring me around their garden, they'll point out the section they and the kids "kinda just did on our own last spring." They seem chagrined by it, ashamed that an expert like me should cast a weary eye onto their heap of plants. Now, if I were a veterinarian and they were showing me the botched liposuction job they and the kids performed on the family wiener dog, uh yeah, then

I could understand some embarrassment but, invariably, this home-made section of their garden is the most refreshing, least narrow-minded, least redundant, least cookie-cutter, carbon-copy slice of real garden to be seen for blocks around. I hover over these "failure" gardens with great joy, reveling in their intuitive correctness. Children and sometimes Moms and Dads plant beautiful gardens because they don't know how . . . not to.

Here in Southern California, where the water is imported from four-hundred miles away, each blade of grass in my front yard is artificial. Every rose petal, false. All the sweet peas, phony. I've got ersatz *Echinacea.* None of the sort of vegetation we have in our yard would be here without water from distant lands—especially the vegetables. When tourists complain about how plastic, affected and unreal life in Los Angeles appears to be, I snicker 'cause they don't even know the half of it. There is no right or wrong way to do a garden here, it's all fantasy, all of it a fairy-tale vision.

Consequently, when I step into gardens I often see collections of plants bought at a store, placed in the ground by the house's original architect or contractor, and tweaked by the tastes of prior and present homeowners with yet more store-bought plants. Rarely do I come across a garden that is homegrown. That's why I love family-project gardens, vegetables coming up as volunteers, wildflowers against the garage, single twelve-foot sunflowers planted by squirrels poking out of the hedge. *Anyone* can buy a garden, stick it in the ground, water and fertilize it on schedule, spray it against pests and diseases, prune it, deadhead it, tear it up and rake it clean when it's "finished" and then go out and buy it again. And buy it again and buy it again. Anyone can do that.

Few people ever learn to let a garden grow. Fewer books will tell you how and that's because it doesn't take much book to relay this information to you . . .

- ~ Clear and stir up some of your yard

- ~ Sprinkle some seeds into this lightly worked soil

- ~ Cover the seeds lightly with rich soil

- ~ Sprinkle the soil gently with water every day
  until sprouts appear

- ⁓ Water the sprouts whenever you think they might need it—not too much, not too little. Gentle.
- ⁓ Watch your garden grow, enjoy it, and help it grow only when it really seems to need a hand.

Undeniably, people enjoy mastering a garden. People love to impose a sense of order, albeit fleeting. True satisfaction can be derived from creating something and having it turn out exactly as it was determined to be. But frankly, in the end, if all you've done is purchase a garden at a garden center, read some books and reaped the inevitable bounty, then, for all of your toil, you will only have peeled the outermost skin of the metaphoric onion, and you will still know less than you would have if you had simply planted a pumpkin seed, watched it wind about wherever it cared to, flowered, fruited and informed your life effortlessly.

Excellent. You now know how to garden. Of course, you didn't need me to tell you that.